D1878896

RURAL EDUCATION

A study of Universalistion of Eduction in India

RURAL EDUCATION

A study of Universalistion of Eduction in India

By

G. Sudarshanam

GYAN

© **Author**

All rights reserved. No part of this work may be reproduced, stored, adapted, or transmitted in any form or by any means, electronic, mechanical, photocopying, micro-filming, recording or otherwise, or translated in any language, without the prior written permission of the copyright owner and the publisher. The book is sold subject to the condition that it shall not, by way of trade or otherwise, be lent, resold, hired out, or otherwise circulated without the prior publisher's written consent in any form of binding or cover other than that in which it is published.

The views and opinions expressed in this book are author(s) own and the facts reported by them have been verified to the extent possible, and the publishers are not in any way liable for the same.

ISBN : 978-81-212-0351-7

Published, 2018

Published by

Gyan Publishing House
5, Ansari Road
Daryaganj, New Delhi-110002
Phone: 011-47034999, 9811692060
www.gyanbooks.com
E-mail: books@gyanbooks.com

Printed at: G. Print Process, Delhi.

Preface

The question of universalisation of elementary education and provision of better educational facilities to people of the country needs to be raised and discussed in the wake of an ongoing debate on new policy trends in Indian education system. This concern is warranted as India has a very large illiterate population now. According to the World Bank estimate by 2007 AD India would have the largest concentration of illiterate populatlon (54.8 pes cent) in the world. The much debated document on 'Challenge of Education' (Ministry of Education, Government of India. 1985) reiterated the urgency and importance of removal of illiteracy in the country. It emphsised taat "if adequate measures are not taken for the spread of education, the chasm of economic disabilities, regional imbalances and social injustic will widen further resulting in building up of disintegrative tensions" (p.4). Therefore, the 'Challenge ol Education' envisaged the attainment of the goal of universalisation of elementary education by 1990. But taking into account the operational difficulties, the National Policy on Education 1986 further postponed the goal to 1955 (p. 12). The National Front Government at the centre was also emphsising on achieving the goal by 1995. This goal which ought to have been achieved in 1960 as per the constitutional directive has been getting postoned again and again.

Kothari Commission traced the causes for failure to achieve universalizátion of education to lack of adequate resources, tremendous increase in population, resistance to education of airls, large number of the children of the backward classes, general poverty of the people and illiteracy and apathy of parents (Report of the Education Commission 1964-66, Ministry of Education, Government of India, New Delhi, 1978, p. 137). The document on 'Challenge of Education' also attributed the failure to the general apathy towards education, poverty, irrelevance of educational content, lack of women teachers and allocation of inadequate resources, (p. 91). One can notice that the two documents with a time gap of more than two decades mentioned the same reasons. This shows that these problems were not tackled for the last two decades or so. The drop-out rate at the elementary level (Classes I-VIII) continues to be above 75 per cent. This rate is much higher among girls, Scheduled Castes and Scheduled Tribes. Many schools lack basic amenities like school building, black boards, library etc. These problems are more alarming in the case of rural arras suffer from low rate of literacy, high rate of drop-outs and a large number of schools lack basic amentities.

In the light of this situation the present study seeks to have an inepth understanding of rural education by going into various details of educational situation in selected villages. The main objective of the study is to find out, how far the environment of education, administrative set-up, physical equipment and attitudes of various groups—teachers, parents, elite, students—towards rural education are conducive to the achievement of policy objective of universalization of education and also the development of rural education. It seeks to examine how structure of education, behaviour of individuals concerned and ecology of educatton influences the educational processes and the policy objective of universalization of elementary edueation. It examined the problem from the point of view of parents, elite, teachers and students. It also seeks to examine the impact of mid-day meal scheme on universalization of elementary education. Thus it attempts to find out the gap between promise and performance of educational system in rural areas.

The scope of the study is confined to the study of administration of education, especially at the field level, It attempts to analyse the problem of education in four schools in three selected villages in the district of Warangal in the Telangana region of Andhra Pradesh. The three villages viz., 'Peta', 'Konda' and 'Kur' (pseudonyms) were having primary, upper primary and secondary schools respectively.

The study is mostly based on primary data. For the purpose of the study the sample taken includes 205 parenss i.e., 10 per cent of the total households in three selected villages ; 50 village elite covering village officials, gram panchayat members, sarpanchas and caste elites of the viliages ; 32 teachers, nearly all the teachers of the four schools in the selected villages ; and 85 students covering fifty per cent of the total strength of classes IX and X of the only secondary school under study, They were interviewed with the help of a structured questionaire. Care was taken to see that all the castes and classes are covered.

In addition to questionarie method, the observation method and informal discussion have also been employed to elicit required information. Discussion were held with concerned officials in education department at the district and block levels. The village schools and their functioding was keenly observed for more than a year and good rapport was develo-with parents, village elite, teachers and students of the villages. This yielded reasonably good results.

For the purpose of analysis of the data the parents were clossified into three classes and three caste groups. While the class analysis is made on the basis of their land, income, agr,cultural implements, crops etc., the caste analysis is based on caste classification made by the Government i.e., forward castes, backward castes, scheduled castes and scheduled tribes. In the case of class divisiou they were divided into rich, middle and poor class.

To supplement primary data the study relies on secondary sources like reports of the Government ank studies conducted by institutions and individuals at various places. Some data collected from the offices of District Educational Officer, Zilla Parishad. Panchayat Samithi, offlce of Deputy Inspector of schools and the schools under study.

This book is an outcome of Ph. D. thesis. Though the field data was collected five years ago, its findidgs are relevant even today. Except adding one or two new sections, one or two class rooms and few more students the basic condition of the schools under study have not changed.

A number of individuals and institutions have helped me in various stages of this work. I am deeply indebted to all of them. I express my deep sense of gratitude to my teacher and research supervisor Prof. G. Haragopal, who took lot of pains in designing and guiding tne work inspite of his tight schedule the heavy responsibilities. He took every care and deep interest,

I express my thaks to my colleagues in the Department for their keen interest in publishing the work. I am also grateful to the University of Hyderabad for financially supporting the publication of the work.

I also express my thanks to Sri Sastry, Sri Narendra Kumar, Sri Gopal, Sri A. Basalingappa and Sri Basha for their help in typing the work. Finally, I express my thanks to my wife and chilnren who eo-operated and encouraged me all through the work.

G. Sudarshanam

1

Catalyst for Socio-economic Change

Education is an essential tool for the advancement of mankind. It works as a catalyst for the socio-economic changes in society. *Enyclopaedia of Britanica* viewed education as 'transmission of the values and accumulated knowledge of society' [1] Education is designed to guide the child in learning a culture, moulding his behaviour in the ways of adulthood, and guiding him towards his eventual role in society.[2] It is conscious social function which began when man started interacting with material reality with the purpose of moulding or changing it to satisfy his needs.[3]

Thus, education embraces a multi-process by which culture and values are transmitted from generation to generation According to a well known sociologist R.K Mukherjee, every education, whatever means and methods it uses, aims at fitting the growing individual for his special role and position in society so as to elicit the best out of him, and at the same time socialising him, through development of proper habits, attitudes and values, so that he enriches and strengthens the cultural pattern.[4]

Broadly speaking, education has two important functions, viz., the conservative and creative. In its conservative function, education helps us in the transmission of cultural values and socially approved behaviour patterns to the younger members of the society. However, the modern human society is characterised by social dynamism. These days, the functions of innovation and change are much prominent than they were in the older society. Therefore, modern education has an added function that is, to inculcate new ideas and thought patterns along with the transmission of established culture and values.[5]

It is in this light, the significance of education is highlighted in the context of developing societies such as India. For the sake of analytical convenience, the impact of education can be studied with reference to these broad spheres of social life—social, political and economic.

Education as an Instrument of Social Change

Social change can be understood as achieving equality of social status to all, greater social participation and acquiring new values of rational thinking. The relevance of education in this field of social change and advancement is increasingly realised by all societies. A.R. Desai an eminent social scientist states that, the significance of education in modern societies cannot be over estimated. Literates and educated people are pre-requisite both for the maintenance and advancement of developing societies. The crucial need of education for the people in various spheres of modern social life—economic, political, social, ethical and others—has been unanimously recognised.[6]

Education being a vital instrument of social change, a developing society like India has to pay serious attention particularly in view of the social transformation that the country is passing through. A system of education suited to the needs for a society committed to modernisation has to keep pace with the demands of both the expansion of knowledge and the accelerated velocity of social change.[7]

In addition, in a developing society which is in the grip of superstition and ignorance, the school is expected to undo what the home and its surroundings had done to the student in the process of early socialisation. Gunnar Myrdal observes that literacy and general knowledge facilitate both children and adults the acquisition of specific skills and may help to bring about a rationalisation of attitudes. In turn, more rational attitudes provide a motivational preparedness that can facilitate the acquisition of literacy, knowledge and skills.[8] "Where a man does his duty rationally and consciously he will be helping himself and the society of which he is a member. There are socially and economically underpriveleged classes which should be made to come up not only in their interest but of the society as a whole. This becomes possible only when the educational and technical gates are opened to all freely."[9]

In this regard, a famous educationist Paulo Frire said that, when an illiterate peasant participates in this sort of educational experience, he comes to a new awareness of self, has a new sense of dignity, and is stirred in a new hope.[10] In the process of learning they discover that, they are creators of culture and that all their work can be creative.[11] And at this stage, they would no longer be willing to be mere objects, responding to changes occurring around them, they are more likely to decide to take upon themselves the struggle to change the structures of society which until now have served to oppress them.[12]

Regarding the social relevance of education V.K.R.V. Rao points out that, education should provide the younger generation with that knowledge which will enable them to explain many things that they see for which quite often irrational mythological explanations are given. He felt, the weight of superstition is the greatest obstacle in the process of economic development, and therefore, education should develop a spirit of rationality, identify a spirit of human solidarity and a feeling of identification with the masses.[13] In this regard the observation made by Alva Mydral, is quite apt. 'What but education can inspire the habit to probe instead of believe, to analyse critically instead of blindly accept, to weight alternatives and choose with eyes open towards the future'.[14] Thus, knowledge increases the power of reasoning and ability to analyse and relate facts and events in their proper sequence, to draw inferences and to apply the conclusions to a given or new situations'.[15]

The school not only occupies a central place in the maintenance of social order in modern societies, it also typifies the way organisations work as agents of social control. Jackson has argued that it is within schools that children learn to live with crowds with the public evaluation of their performance and with the exercise of power by stranger.[16] As people and their ideas become adapted to the new ways of life so will the schools ; they in their turn will be one of the chief agencies through which change will be brought about, and this in turn will affect the economy of the whole country.[17]

Education as an Instrument of Political Development

Political development can be understood as achieving equality of opportunities to all in the political field and greater participation of people in the political process. Education plays a crucial role in this process of political development. Political silence of the people will have an adverse impact on development. So education helps in removing political immaturity of the people. Paulo Freire, says that, the greater the political immaturity of the people the more easily they can be manipulated by those who do not want to lose their power.[18] For, those who are engaged in learning to read and write, come to a new awareness of self-hood and begin to look critically at the social situation in which they find themselves, often take the initiative in acting to transform the society that has denied them this opportunity of participation.[19] It is further expected that, the illiterate and poor can rise to their own liberation through literacy, dialogue and action.[20] Education conscientizes the large illiterate and ignorant masses who are suffering from the 'culture of silence'.[21]

Referring to the significance of education in moulding the political character of people, in developing countries, Gunnar Myrdal observed that whenever there was a liberation movement, educational reform stood high on the agenda.[22] It has become the common characteristic of all modernising movements, whether revolutions or independent movements in

Russia, Japan, China, the African countries, the Islamic World, and South East Asia have all had at the starting point of their struggle a fairly numerous and differentiated educated elite.[23]

Education is more meaningful in the Third World countries because democratic institutions cannot succeed without education. For, democracy functions only when the people are informed and have thirst for knowledge and exchange of ideas.[24]

Education is the only instrument to effect a political change. The commitment to secularism, socialism and democracy will be realised when there is development in human resources in terms of knowledge and skills, it should impart attitudes and values against oppressive economic, social and political forces.

Education as a Catalyst for Economic Prosperity

Economic development of a nation cannot be separated from the educational level of the nation. Education becomes more necessary for economy and is linked closely to it as a major mediator between manpower demand and labour supply.[25] Formal education plays a leading role in the formation of human resource development. In fact, one of the main functions of the education system is to supply qualified manpower to meet the demands of national economy and thereby contribute to its growth.

The developing societies which have been poor and stagnant for centuries are in a state of revolt against poverty, disease, ignorance and exploitation by stronger nations. Further, they are no longer inclined to entrust their future exclusively to the forces of the market, the whims of nature or the judgement of colonial rulers.[26] The realisation of this objective depends upon the educational level of the people of the nation. Thus education is the key that unlocks the door to economic modernisation. Paulo Freire put it succintly when he observed "if millions of men are illiterate, starved for letters, thirsty for words, the word must be brought to them to save them from 'hunger' and 'thirst'".[27]

A literate agricultural community can read and write a

material, adopt better agricultural practices easily and quickly for which an illiterate has to depend upon personal resources. *Taiwan has achieved a great* deal of increase in agricultural productivity because of the exposure of *its agriculturists* to education. Japan's phenomenal post-war growth would have been impossible if it was not for the fact that 98 per cent of her people can read and write.[28]

Coming to India which is predominantly an agricultural country, the spread of education can stimulate the agricultural production because, the cultivator is now involved in a transaction in which an illiterate man is at a great disadvantage. Schemes to improve agricultural methods and to improve the general conditions of rural poor depend crucially for their success upon the spread of education amongst the masses which would ultimately raise the level of productivity, improve the occupational skills of the individual and the quality of labour force. Thus education results in increased innovativeness and more effective performance of given tasks because of improved abilities.[29] For modern education affects the economy in a number of ways, not only does it increase the flow of skills, but enables people to acquire new techniques. Moreover, it has the potential to destroy the traditional attitudes which impede the progress.[30]

Education and Overall Development

Apart from the above mentioned aspects there are many other advantages of education. Emphasising on the importance of education in India, the Education Commission states that—'the destiny of India is now being shaped in her class-rooms'.[31] This, the Commission felt is not mere rhetoric. In a world based on science and technology, it is education that determines the level of prosperity, welfare and security of the people. The quality and number of persons coming out of our schools and colleges will depend on our success in the great enterprise of national reconstruction whose principal objective is to raise the standards of living of our people.[32] The Education Commission felt that, the change on a grand scale is possible only through education. It further envisaged a direct link between education, national development and prosperity and emphasised that this is possible only when the national system of education is properly organised from both qualitative and quantitative points of view. Education is a double-edged sword which can be used to promote social justice or perpetuate injustice. History shows numerous instances where small social groups and elite used education as a prerogative of their rule and as a tool for maintaining their hegemony and perpetuating the values upon which it has rested. On the other hand, a social and cultural revolution has been brought about in a system where equality of educational opportunity is provided and education is consciously used for developmental purposes.[33]

As the fundamental task of education is to help men and their societies to reach the state of critical consciousness, it follows that education can no more be considered as an isolated activity, to be carried out in a vaccum. It becomes part and parcel of the complex phenomena that make a man and promote the attainment of the goal and ideals which are conceived in terms of the liberation of man and his community. Education, being a sub-system, is closely dependent on the larger socio-political system.[34]

Keeping this growing importance of education in mind the International Commission on Development of Education has an idea of life long education as the key-stone of the learning society.[35] Every individual must be in a position to keep learning throughout his life.

In fact, the concept of an Open University has come only to make the learning system more comprehensive and integrate the components to varied forms of open learning systems.[36] And this Open University learning system will definitely lead to the further spread of education in rural areas.

In the words of Louis Malassis, there is a dialectical relationship between society and education ; education is both the product of society and in certain circumstances, a factor making for social change.[37] While education is necessary for the promotion of economic development, education is also essential for enjoying the fruits of life. One needs to be educated in order to be a better man, to have a richer life and to have a more integrated personality.[38]

Education helps a person in the unfolding of his personality by bringing forth and revealing the potential qualities in him. Education develops the mind, the physique, the sense and the skills and nourishes the thinking qualities of the learner. It affords a means for a person to earn his livelihood and also serve the society in several ways.[39]

Education in India

After highlighting the overall significance of education, here, an attempt is made to discuss the development of education in India and some of the problems it has been facing from the beginning.

(1) *Historical Perspective*

A brief presentation of some of the historical aspects will help us in understanding the present and the future. As far as the history of education is concerned, it can be traced to the invention of writing.

The invention of reading and writing—that is to say, the conventional visual symbols to present the sounds of a spoken language—goes back to the remote times of pre-history. Next to man's discovery of the art of using articulate sound to express and communicate thought, it is perhaps the most decisive and far reaching achievement of the human mind.[40] J.P. Naik, an eminent educationist observes—'the school as an institution was born at the stage in social development when division of labour became pronounced and the need to create special institutions and special functionaries for several categories of social activities began to be felt.[41] For instance, knowledge or skills developed to such an extent that their preservation, promotion, and diffusion could not be managed through individual or non-formal channels. It was found necessary to create special groups as teachers and the formal school as an institution to perform these functions. The process began in most societies with the development and accumulation of sacred religious literature which made it necessary to establish formal schools and to train up a group of individuals in every generation to preserve and disseminate this knowledge and also to add to it to the extent possible or desirable. Thus arose the priestly class and formal school system where young persons could be trained to join and sustain the class.[42]

In Indian traditional society, which shows the beginning of caste hierarchy and cultural inequality, educational system was greatly influenced by its hierarchical tradition. In this society, the division of labour was simple and the role of education was limited to serve the interest of a favoured class of the traditional society.[43] The content of education was esoteric and the classical languages were used as the medium of instruction. It was the preserve of mainly those who were superior in terms of caste and class positions, the 'twice-born' castes. In this system some elements like equality, rationality, specialisation and secularism could not receive any important place.[44] With the advent of British rule in India, the traditional type of education was changed and a new system of education was established. The most formative period of educational changes during the colonial rule started from the time of Warren Hastings (1773) to the time of Woods Despatch of 1854. During this period, it was thought that the British rule required trained Indians of only upper classes to man the lower positions in their politico-administrative organisations, but win the confidence of those who lost their political influence, and make them loyal to the British government. And it was further thought that, the British culture was superior to the Indian culture and therefore, the Indians had to be 'civilised.'

Hence to achieve the above goals, the British established educational institutions which were meant for a small group of Indians from upper classes to train them for top subordinate positions of the British Administration. This was further strengthened by the ideas of Macauly, who wanted to produce through these educational institutions, persons who are 'Indian in blood and colour, but English in taste, in opinion, in morals and in intellect'.[45] This policy, pursued by Britishers succeeded in producing a troop of clerks and bureaucrats who were competent enough to handle administration.

The British educational policy strengthened stratification and widened the gap between the ruling elite and the ruled masses ; the English knowing people became a class by themselves ; education became highly loaded with English literature and language, European tradition and science, and education became very expensive.[46]

It was after 1854 that, gradual attempts were made to popularise education among masses. The Indian Education Commission (Hunter Commission) appointed in 1882. stressed on the need for special attention to be given to weaker sections of society and need for expansion of educational facilities. With the result considerable expansion in school education took place during the years 1882 to 1902. For instance, the total number of secondary schools increased from 3,916 in 1882 to 5,129 in 1902 with an increase in the number of students from 214,077 to 590,129. But education remained western-oriented and the indigeneous schools almost disappeared by 1902. This expansion resulted in the organisation of the department of education. The system of grants-in-aid also came into existence. Responsibility for promoting education, was given to various agencies, such as the missionaries, local bodies and private institutions like Ramakrishna Mission, Arya Samaj, etc.

The idea of popularising education among Indian people received much attention during anti-colonial movement. At that time the literacy rate was very low (6 per cent). The Congress Party was constantly demanding the spread of education. Gopal Krishna Gokhale (1911) pleaded for free and compulsory education. But the idea was rejected by the government on financial grounds. The Hartog Committee (1929) expressed its concern for raising the educational standards and liberal curriculum.[47] Compulsory education was introduced during 1936-37, but only in urban areas and its enforcement was far from satisfactory.

In the year 1937, Mahatma Gandhi's scheme of Basic Education was introduced. The main objectives of the scheme were removal of illiteracy and increase in national consciousness among the people. The scheme was self supporting and mass-oriented. There was phenomenal growth of the institutions of basic education since 1938 to the Third Five Year Plan in India.[48]

In the year 1944, a new scheme known as Sargent Plan (John Sargent was the then Educational Adviser) was submitted and accepted by the Central Advisory Board of Education. It contained a detailed account of education from nursery to university level. For primary education, the report adopted the scheme of Basic Education with some modifications. For Secondary Education, it recommended two types of high schools i.e., Academic and Technical. Academic Schools will impart instruction in Arts and Pure Science, and Technical High Schools will provide training in the applied sciences and industrial subjects. But this scheme was criticised as too utopian to be implemented.

In the 20th century, there was an unprecedented expansion of education at all levels particularly, the secondary schools rose from 5,493 in 1901-02 to 13,305 in 1937-38 to 17,031 in 1945-46. This rapid expansion may be attributed to the great social and political awakening that heralded the struggle for freedom and was mainly achieved through private enterprise.[49] Commenting on British education policy in India, Hampton (1943) felt that, "the secondary school system suffers from arrested development, it has failed to keep pace with the changes—social, political, economic and industrial. Schools are weighed down by the incubus of Matriculation, and fettered by governing regulation ; courses are bookish and theoretical and provide little to attract pupils with a practical turn of mind ; the excessive use of English as the medium of instruction places a severe psychological burden on both pupils and teachers—it stifles individuality, encourages memorisation and makes instruction lifeless and mechanical ; scientific and practical subjects are neglected and inadequate provision is made for out-door games and recreational activities. The whole system is rigid and inelastic and is characterised by a dull and monotonous uniformity."[50] Such was the policy and nature of education in India during the British period.

(2) *Education in Independent India : Policy and Performance*

A new era in the history of education was started in India with its attainment of Independence in the year 1947. For analytical purposes, developments in education in the post-independence period can be presented under the following heads—

(*i*) *Constitutional Obligations* : Article 45 of the Indian Constitution under Directive Principles of State Policy lays down "The State shall endeavour to provide within a period of ten years from the commencement of this Constitution, free and compulsory education to all children until they complete the age of fourteen years." With regard to the education of weaker sections, the Constitution (Article 46) further envisaged that— "the state shall promote with special care the educational and economic interests of the weaker sections of the people, and particularly of the Scheduled Castes and Scheduled Tribes and shall protect them from social injustices and all forms of exploitation."

(*ii*) *Major Developments in Post-Independence Period*: When India attained freedom, it had only 5,297 secondary schools with 870,000 pupils. This meant, not even one youth from every 20 in the age-group of 14-17 was in school. There were 12,843 middle schools with two million pupils. This meant, one child out of every eleven in the age-group of 11-14 was enrolled in the school. The number of primary schools constituted 172, 661 with fourteen million pupils. This implied that only one child out of every three in the age group of 6-11 was in school.[51] The percentage of literacy was only 14 and the total educational expenditure was just about Rs. 570 million or less than half a per cent of the national income. It was this challenging situation which the nation was called upon to reform when it kept its tryst with destiny in 1947.[52]

After Independence, though the policy of providing education to all children in the age group of 6-14 was essentially sound, its implementation has been very bad. The result is, we are far away from the goal, which we ought to have reached in the year 1960. The enthusiasm, however, soon waned. The first plan itself did not appear very enthusiastic about the provision of facilities for primary education as it was conditioned by the idea of 'quick returns'. The Second Plan, though it was in favour of primary education opted for the operation of free and compulsory education to a limited area. The subsequent plans failed to provide sufficient importance and funds to primary education.

The system of basic education, which was accepted as the national pattern of education at the primary level was gradually given up by the end of the Second Five Year Plan.

The expansion of secondary education has been greater than that of elementary education. The number of secondary schools have been increased from 6,682 in 1949-50 to 16,000 in 1960-61, and touched 40,000 in 1973-74.

One of the significant developments in secondary education was the appointment of Secondary Education Commission under the Chairmanship of Dr. A.L. Mudaliar in 1952. The Commission felt that, secondary education, grown out of British period was too academic and provided a single track leading to university education. As a remedy, the commission recommended diversification of secondary education, through establishment of multipurpose schools[53] which would provide terminal course in technology, commerce, agriculture, fine arts and home science. With the result, about 2,115 such multipurpose schools were created by the end of second plan.

Another landmark in the field of education was the appointment of Indian Education Commission (1964-66) under the Chairmanship of Dr. D.S Kothari. It recommended work experience which involves participation of students in some form of productive work [54] It also recommended a common school system of public education which will cover all parts of the country and all stages of school education and strive to provide equality of access to all children.[55] Though the recommendations of this commission were carefully considered by the government, they have not been implemented.

With all these efforts, India could attain the literacy rate of 36.74 per cent in 1981, which was only 16.67 per cent in 1951. However, India has failed to make substantial progress towards universal education for children upto the age of 14.

While the network of schooling has been provided, covering ·96 per cent of the rural population with primary schooling facilities within walkable distance, nearly 50 million out-of-school children are to be enrolled to achieve universalisation of education.[56] But the major problem in achieving this target is the huge rate of drop-outs which is of the order of over 60 per cent in classes I to V and 77 per cent in classes I to VIII.[57] Unless this problem is solved, universalisation is not possible.

The position of primary school buildings, as revealed by the third and fourth educational survey is very dismal. There exists a huge backlog of (nearly 40%) school buildings to be built. Similarly the supply position (equipment) of these schools is very appealing. Nearly 95 per cent to 98 per cent of the budgetary provision on elementary education is spent on the salaries of teachers and very little remains for the non-teaching expenses and almost nothing for the programme of quality improvement at the elementary stage. Nearly 30 per cent of the total number of primary schools are single-teacher schools.[58]

There is general dissatisfaction regarding the secondary and higher education systems because of their rigidities, restrictions of educational choice and their emphasis being general rather than vocational. Their general irrelevance to students and falling standards is the most critical aspect of education.

(*iii*) *Finances* : The proportion of financial allocation to Education to the total outlay has been decreasing from plan to plan. It was 7.6 per cent in the First, 6.0 per cent in the Second, 6.8 per cent in the Third, 5.1 per cent in the Fourth only 4.6 per cent in the Fifth Plan,[59] and it was further reduced in the Sixth Plan.[60] It is pertinent to point out here that out of this meagre allocations to education, very little is spent on school education and more than half is spent on higher and technical education in every plan. While these were some of the problems faced by Indian education, the government has failed to evolve a suitable policy to achieve substantial progress in education. However, it has made some efforts to evolve a policy on education. A brief presentation of these efforts is made here.

Educational Policy in India

In 1968, the Government of India formulated the national policy of education. This was the result of a wide range of discussions on education after the submission of a report by the Indian Education Commission (1964-66). A brief account of the National Policy as far as school education is concerned, is discussed here.[61]

(i) Free and compulsory education for all children upto the age of 14 should be provided at the earliest possible date and suitable programme should be developed to reduce the prevailing wastage and stagnation in schools,

(ii) Teacher education, particularly in-service education should receive high priority. Teachers must be accorded an honoured place in society,

(iii) The energetic development of Indian language and literature is a 'Sin qua non' for educational and cultural development. The three language formula should be adopted, at secondary stage, i.e., the child should learn the language of his region, Hindi or another Indian language, if the language of his region is Hindi. It was decided that English and Hindi should become the link languages,

(iv) Regional imbalances should be corrected and good educational facilities be provided in rural and backward areas. To promote social cohesion and national integration, a common school system should be adopted,

(v) The school and the community should be brought closer through suitable programme of mutual service and support. Science education and research should be an integral part of general education till the end of the school stage,

(vi) At secondary level, facilities for technical and vocational education need to be increased, diversified and related closely to employment opportunities,

(vii) A broadly uniform educational structure of 10+2+3 should be adopted in all parts of the country.

Apart from these features, the policy also made an important declaration that 'the reconstruction of education on these lines will need additional outlay. The aim should be gradually to increase the investment in education so as to reach a level of expenditure of six per cent of the national income as early as possible'. This ambitious target required a doubling of the roughly three per cent of national income devoted to education.

After 10 years of the declaration of National Policy, keeping in view the foregoing developments, it was reviewed and a 'Draft National Policy on Education, 1978' was circulated by the central government and was placed before Parliament in 1979. This draft policy was only a modification of the 1968 policy, no major changes were made in it. However, greater attention was drawn to the aims of education, the education of SCs and STs, and 12+3 or 12+2 pattern of education.[62]

New Education Policy 1986

After the draft policy of 1979, it was only in 1985 a fresh attempt was made to evolve a policy on education to suit the changing requirements of society. 'Challenge of Education' a document issued by the Ministry of Education, Government of India, was only a confession of failures in Indian education. This document, released for public debate, was very critical of the education system in India.[63] It also proposed a new policy on education. Based on this document, the Government of India formulated a new policy called the 'National Policy on Education—1986'. Some of the aspects of the new education policy which are relevant for the present study are briefly presented here.[64]

This policy has emphasised, among many other things, on the establishment of a national system of education with 10+2+3 structure. The national system of education will be based on a national curricular framework which contains a common core along with other components. The new policy also emphasised on the removal of disparities and equalising educational opportunities and on the need for a special focus on the educational development of Scheduled Castes, Schedule Tribes and Women.

It gave greater importance to adult education, eradication of illiteracy, particularly in the 15-35 age group. It emphasised on involving central and state governments, educational institutions, voluntary organisations and use of mass media like radio and T.V. in the task of eradication of illiteracy.

The new policy has given importance to launching a systematic programme of non-formal education for school dropouts and working children who cannot attend formal schools. Use of modern technological aids to improve the non-formal education programme was also emphasised. The new policy also laid stress on an integrated approach to early childhood care and pre-primary education. The new education policy thus, resolved that by 1995 all children will be provided free and compulsory education upto 14 years of age.

Another important area, where the new policy gave greater importance and attracted the attention of many people is the establishment of pace-setting schools. The policy mentioned that the pace-setting schools will be established in various parts of the country to help children with special talent. The broad aim will be to serve the objective of excellence, coupled with equity and social justice. (This proposal led to the establishment of Navodaya Schools in many parts of the country). Some of the other aspects that the new policy emphasised were vocationalisation of higher secondary education, strengthening of open learning system at higher education level, de-linking degrees from jobs, development of the new pattern of the Rural University on the lines of Mahatma Gandhi's ideas on education, encouraging technical and management education, use of modern educational technology and establishment of District Institutes of Education and Training (DIET), to organise pre-service and in-service courses for elementary school teachers and for the personnel working in non-formal and adult education. After discussing the educational policy, we shall further examine the practical problems faced by the Indian education system.

Problems of Indian Education

Even after 40 years of Independence, inspite of different

policy pronouncements on education, India is far away from the constitutional and national policy goals of universalisation of elementary education. India could not attain fully any of the principles laid down in its policies. On the other hand, the claim of the government, i.e., near eighty per cent enrolment in primary schools is believed to be inflated.[65] On the one hand, India had over 70 million learners at different levels of schooling, perhaps the largest in the world excluding China. But on the other, India has the distinction of having the largest number of illiterates.[66] One will be grieved to note that about half of the total illiterates of the world live in India.[67] India had 213 million illiterates in 1951, 333 million in 1961 and 387 million in 1971 and 424 million in 1981. What is more alarming is that the number of illiterate children in the age group of 5-14 also rose in these decades. These unfortunate millions of illiterates belong to what is known as the weaker sections of society who stand below the poverty line.[68]

There are several reasons for this failure of education system.

(i) *Education and Social System* : Education and the social system are closely inter-linked and their mutual interaction is critical to an understanding of this relationship. Therefore, we should understand the failures of educational system through the social angle. Change in or through the educational system is not possible without prior changes in the social structure.[69] In a stratified society, the education system does not allow the poorer class to enter it. Most surveys by sociologists have brought out the point, rather forcefully, that a majority of students in our country are from the upper and middle strata of the society.[70] J.P. Naik observed that, the present education system is class based, as it mainly emphasises on higher education, which benefits the 'haves' rather than the 'have-nots'.[71] The entire educational system has been oriented to meet the requirements of the top one-third of the population, the well-to-do sections and the upper and middle classes in urban and rural areas—and the interests of poor, constituting the lower two-thirds of the population, have by and large been ignored.[72] In fact, the educational system in India did not make a radical departure from the one which the British had implemented earlier.

A.R. Desai observed that education continues to be the preserve of small richer sections and works as a powerful instrument of perpetuation of inequalities.[73]

Available studies have shown that, students from under-privileged groups tend to attend inferior or less prestigious institutions.[74] Thus, membership of the affluent upper strata tends to help students from this strata to get a better quality of education, admission into the desired professional courses and to exploit other avenues to improve their merit and get through public examinations.

The upper strata in the Indian society continues to operate in a manner that is obstructive of restoration of equality in terms of participation by different groups of people with the result, there is no relevance of education to local needs and media of instruction caters to selective groups of our population.[75] Upper classes know that education is a powerful instrument for social transformation and that any attempt is thus likely to jeopardize their superior position that they hold in the Indian society. The victims of these oppressions perpetuated by the upper strata in the Indian society are largely economically weaker sections, consisting among others women, Scheduled Castes and Scheduled Tribes.[76]

Thus, education became a monopoly of the children belonging to families which hold economic resources and command social prestige. The rest of the population laboured for the upkeep of this upper class, worked for them in the fields and attended to their comforts. Children belonging to lower strata joined their elders for the service of the elites at a very tender age. Education was not in their realm.[77]

In this context it is not out of place to examine the views of Bertrand Russel who points out that, in the context of education, it is the social position of the fathers that determines the status of children. Thus is in any society, where class distinction exists, children are respected not solely on account of their own merits, but also on account of the wealth and status of their fathers. The children of rich acquire a belief that they are superior to the children of poor, and an attempt is made to make the children of poor to think themselves inferior to the children of rich.[78]

(ii) *Structural Deficiencies* : Apart from the social causes, there are certain deficiencies in the Indian education system itself. In this regard, J.P. Naik pointed out certain deficiencies in the traditional model of education which India has been following now. These defects are also one of the reasons for not reaching the goals of universal elementary education. He felt that the traditional model of the development of primary education was essentially meant for the well-to-do-class which appreciates the value of education and is also in a position to feed, clothe and equip their children to attend schools on a whole-time basis. It has, therefore, a built-in-bias in favour of the education of the classes and built-in antagonism for the education of the masses. It is this basic issue which often goes unrecognised and needs clarification.[9]

The defects[80] pointed out by J.P. Naik, in the existing primary schools are ;

(a) *Single-point entry* : In this system, a child is expected to enter the primary education system at about the age of six in class-I. A child who missed to enter the system, may not be allowed to enter at a later age say 11 or 14. Even if the child is admitted, the admission is made only in Class-I and this grown-up child is required to sit along other young children, learn the same lessons, and at the same speed. This is usually boring to him and often runs away from school and becomes a drop-out. For this he suggested a multiple-point entry system in separate classes.

(b) *Sequential character* : The existing primary schools are also a sequential system in the sense that a child is expected to complete one class every year and goes to the next class after passing the annual examination. Many children who fail to pass the examination at the end of the year are, therefore, detained in the same class as repeaters, resulting in large scale stagnation. This is disadvantageous to the children who are admitted late. Hence, Naik suggested that, grown-up children should be allowed to complete education in much shorter period.

(c) *Full time instruction* : Another important aspect of the existing system is that they only provide full-time institutional instruction. This system is extremely antagonistic to the interests of the masses who are so poor that their children are compelled to work at home or outside and to add to the meagre family budget. This results in either discouragement to go to school or leads to drop-out, sooner than the later. This results in larger scale wastage in school education. To prevent this, he suggested part-time education to suit the convenience of children.

(d) *Exclusive utilisation of professional teachers* : The present education uses the services of full-time professional teachers only. This is done in the name of standards. But it creates problems like continuous increase in costs. Hence, it is suggested to fully utilise all the teaching resources available in the local community, the services of part-time local teachers and even of senior students for promoting instruction in the primary schools. And girls who are required to look after young children should be encouraged to bring them to the schools.

(iii) *Defective planning* : Inspite of planning in the country, we could not achieve universalisation. Plan after plan could not make sufficient allocations for education and they have not paid much attention to it. For the failure of these plans in education, J.P. Naik in one of his studies[81] has pointed out several causes. The major weakness of our planning system is top heaviness. So much is done at the top and so little at the bottom. It is mostly done in the Planning Commission and to some extent in the state education department. There are no district plans, and no plans for individual educational institutions. Since the educational process takes place in class-rooms, the core of any plan should be prepared by each educational institution. The top oriented plan tends to be expenditure oriented. And this process of planning from above does not involve the willing and enthusiastic participation of inspecting officers, teachers, parents and students. Hence Planning should be from below and known to all and it should provide adequate freedom to schools to make decisions.

(iv) *Education under Panchayati Raj* : It is being increasingly realised that the association of local leaders with the management of primary schools is desirable for recognising local conditions and aspirations and for on-the-spot supervision and control. It is also being recognised that if such association tends to involve the teachers in local politics, it may do more harm than good. Thus the possibility of a depoliticised zone seems to require association of local political leaders with the management of primary schools on the one hand, and protection of the schools against appropriation by local politicians on the other.[82]

It is in this context we have to understand the relationship between education and Panchayati Raj. In a study made by Inamdar, it is found that, the process of spread of schooling facilities has received a momentum with the association of Panchayati Raj bodies with educational administration. But frequent changes in the staff disturbed the school organisation as well as the relation of the school with community. The interest that non-officials evinced in the matter of teachers' transfer is the root cause for this defect.[83] Therefore, this study suggested the constitution of district school boards and taluka school committees with full financial resources and administrative powers and independent local authority to correct such defects.

A study made by Iqbal Narain and others, while appreciating the transfer of education to the democratic institutions, discusses the difficulties of dual control-administrative control by Panchayati Raj bodies and technical control by government department.[84] Iqbal Narain observed that transfers appear to be the most common method of political reward or victimisation ; those transferred against their wishes suffer expenses, inconvenience and psychological upset.[85]

(v) *Drop-outs and stagnation* : The drop-out and stagnation have become the major impedements in achieving the goal of universal education in rural areas. Regarding the extent of wastage due to this problem, several surveys made by various organisations (NCERT. State Governments, University Departments) and individuals indicate the incidence of these problems.

In 1966, the Indian Education Commission stated that wastage was to the extent of 56 per cent for boys and 62 per cent for girls. And about two-thirds of this wastage occurs in class-I.[86] J.P. Naik pointed out that, even now out of every 100 children enrolled in class-I, only about 40 reach class V and about 25 reach class-VIII. About half of the total wastage occurs in class-I itself.[87] The document on 'Challenge of Education' (1985) also recognised the fact that there is high drop-out rate (classes I-VIII) which continues to be above 75 per cent. There is every possibility of children who dropped at early primary stages lapsing into illiterates.[88] The Stagnation Index figures given by Indian Education Commission are 40.3 per cent for boys and 47.1 per cent for girls in class-I. Similar figures in class-II are 26.6 for boys and 33.1 for girls. For class III the figures are further reduced to 22.6 for boys and 26.6 for girls. It is a sad picture to find that a good number of students enrolled in class-I continue to remain in the same class for two to three years. It takes seven to nine years for some students to pass class-V.[89]

Reasons for drop-outs

Regarding the causes for this large scale wastage, a study published as early as in 1922, recognised poverty as the main cause of non-attendance and of withdrawal of children from village schools. The employment of child labour was also wide spread.[90] The Indian Education Commission 1964-66, also agreed that about 65 per cent of the wastage is due to poverty. The first and second survey of Research in Education (Edited by M.B. Buch, Baroda, 1974, and 1979) brought out several studies on this aspect.[91] Other studies[92] conducted later, point out that the main cause for this situation is poverty, for the largest number of drop-outs are from poorer sections of the society. The other causes include general illiteracy of parents and lack of proper awareness among them, the opposition from the vested interests in the villages like landlords and richer sections, the practice of child marriages in the villages, lack of physical facilities in schools, lack of extra curricular activities, irregular teachers, teachers not staying in the village etc. Single-teacher schools which get closed frequently also contribute to the drop-out problem. Other causes are, frequent transfers of teachers, lack of middle school and high school education in several villages and the poor quality of incentives provided by the government. Another important reason is the parental preference to send children for agricultural work during the peak season.

(vi) *Irrelevant curriculum, lack of trained teachers and lack of accommodation* : Apart from the above mentioned problems, irrelevant curriculum lack of accomodation in rural schools, lack of competent and adequate number of teachers, dual policy-private and public—with regard to educational institutions, large number of single-teacher schools, etc., are some of the other problems associated with the system of Indian education.

J.P. Naik maintains[93] that there has been an over emphasis on uniformity of curriculum in all primary schools-urban as well as rural and the net result of this trend is that it has made impossible to relate the curriculum to the local environment.

Lack of adequate number of teachers requires the existing teachers of the schools to look after unmanageable number of pupils in a single class or they are required to look after more than one class simultaneously. This adversely affects the quality of teachers. They find it almost difficult to provide individual attention to each pupil.[94]

Lack of adequate number of trained teachers is also another important problem. In a study it was found that, nearly 29.3 per cent English teachers are untrained and poor knowledge on the part of the teachers caused the fall in the standards of learning English.[95] In another survey it was revealed that, existing conditions did not permit the students adequate freedom of choice of their subject. Added to it inadequate pool of competent and devoted teachers, poor library facilities, absence of play grounds and poor physical education programme rendered education porrer in quality.[96]

Yet another study regarding single-teacher schools points out that the teachers have to handle a group of children of different ages, abilities, intensity and stages of learning, so that they form one educational whole and most of their difficulties arise from the fact that he has to teach as many as six or seven subjects.[97]

Summing-Up

The above discussion reveals that education is a very important factor for the socio-economic and political development of any nation. It is more important for a developing country like India. But it can be derived from the above discussion that the Indian education system which evolved from British colonial system did not make a major dent in the post-Independence period. Even after 40 years of Independence, the constitutional objective of universalisation of elementary education is not achieved. Now it is postponed to 1995. Indian education system suffers from certain major problems. There is in-built class bias in the system which only helps the educational development of rich but definitely not the poor. The Plan allocation ratio for education decreased constantly from First Five Year Plan to the present. The schools suffer from inadequate physical facilities, ill-prepared teachers, high incidence of drop-out and wastage, irrelevant curriculum and many other problems. Against this background, the present study seeks to probe further into the concrete problems in the organisation and working of rural educational institutions.

REFERENCES

1. *The New Encyclopaedia of Britanica*, Halen Hemingway, Benton, Chicago, Vol. 6, 1977, p. 316.
2. *Ibid.*
3. Rashid Azer, Education Perception, *Seminar*, No. 88, December, 1966, pp. 25-30.
4. Radha Kamal Mukherjee, *The Social Structure of Values*, S. Chand and Co., New Delhi, 1965, pp. 312-13.
5. G.S. Bhatnagar, *Education and Social Change*, The Minerva Associates, Calcutta, 1972, pp. 4-5.
6. A.R. Desai, *Rural Sociology in India*, Popular Prakashan, Bombay, 1978, p. 65

7. M.V. Rajagopal, *Kothari Commission on School Education, Recapitulation and Review*, Telugu Vidyarthi Prachuranalu, Machilipatnam, 1967, pp. 7-8.
8. Gunnar Myrdal. *Asian Drama-An Inquiry into the Poverty of Nations*, Abridged by Seth S. King, Allen lane the Penguine Press ; London, 1972, pp. 313-314.
9. B.R.K. Rau, Education and Welfare, *Khadi Gramodyog*, Vol. xx, No. 8, May 1974, pp. 462-504.
10. Paulo Friere, *Pedagogy of the Oppressed*, Penguin Education, Middlesex. 1980, pp. 8-12.
11. *Ibid.*, p. 13.
12. *Ibid.*
13. V.K.R.V. Rao, *Education and Human Resource Development*, Allied Publishers, Bombay, 1966, p. 61.
14. Alva Myrdal, *The Power of Education*, in Emmet John Hugh (ed), *Education in World Perspective*, Lancer Books, New York, 1965, p. 132.
15. S.C. Goel, *Education and Economic Growth in India*. The MacMillan Company of India, Delhi, 1975, p. 11.
16. M.D. Shipman, *Education and Modernisation*, Faber and Faber, London, 1971, pp. 51-52.
17. John Vaizey, *Education for Tomorrow*, Penguin, London. 1966, p. 11.
18. Paulo Freire, *Pedagogy of the Oppressed, op. cit.*, p. 116.
20. *Ibid.*, p. 9.
26. *Ibid.*,
21. Paulo Freire maintained that, 'In the culture of silence the masses are 'mute' that is, they are prohibited from creatively taking part in the transformation of their society and therefore, prohibited from being', see Paulo Freire, *Cultural Action for Freedom*, Penguin, London, 1977, p. 30.
22. Gunnar Myrdal Education Reforms in Underdeveloped Countries, in A.B. Shan (ed.,) *Social Context of Education : Essays in Honour of J.P. Naik*, Allied Publishers, 1975, p. 69.
23. Aparna Basu, *The Growth of Education and Political Development in India, 1898-1920*, Oxford University Press, New Delhi 1974, p. 235.
24. Sateswari Saxena : *Educational Planning in India : A Study in Approach and Methodology*, Sterling Publishers, New Delhi, 1979, p. 5.
25. *International Encyclopaedia of Social Sciences*. The MacMillan Company and the Free Press, Vol. 4, 1968, p. 510.
26. Fredrick Harbison and C.A. Myere, *Education, Manpower and Economic Growth Strategies of Human Resources Development*, Macgraw Hill, New York, 1964.

27. Paulo Freire, *Cultural Action for Freedom, op. cit.*, p. 24.
28. A.S. Rama Swamy, Education for Higher Productivity, *Kurukshetra*, Vol. 20, No. 2 October, 16, 1971, pp. 16-17.
29. K. Venkata Subramaniam. *Education and Economic Development in India : Tamil Nadu—A Case Study*, Frank Brothers, Delhi, 1980, p. 4.
30. John Vaizey, *Education for Tomorrow, op. cit.*, p. 11.
31. Report of the Education Commission 1964-65, *Education and National Development*, Ministry of Education, Government of India, New Delhi, 1966 p. 1.
32. *Ibid.*.
33. Report of the Education Commission 1964-66. *op. cit.*, p. 4-5.
34. Majid Rahnema, "Iran", in Suresh Chandra Gosh (ed.,) *Educational Strategies in Developing Countries*, Sterling Publishers, New Delhi, 1976, p. 26.
35. International Commission on the Development of Education *'learning to be*, UNESCO, Sterling Publishers, New Delhi, 1973, p. 181.
36. *Towards an Open Learning System*, Report of the Committee on the Establishment of an Open University, Hyderabad, 1982, p. 23. The various forms of open learning systems are : part-time studies, adult and continuing education, studying through audio-visual aids like television, radio and print media etc.
37. Louis Malassis, *The Rural Word : Education and Development*, Croom Helm, London, 1976, p. 20.
38. V.K.R.V. Rao, *Education and Human Resource Development, op. cit.*, p. 58.
39. R.N. Joshi, *Education Elsewhere and Here*, Bharatiya Vidya Bhavan, Bombay, 1979. p. 1.
40. Charles Jeffries, *Illiteracy : A World Problem*, Pall Mall Press, London, 1967, p. 4.
41. J.P. Naik, *Some Perspectives on Non-formal Education*, Allied Publishers, New Delhi, 1977, pp. 3-4.
42. *Ibid.*, p. 4.
43. Ehsnul Haq, *Education and Political Culture in India*, Sterling Publishers, New Delhi, 1977, pp 3-4. 1981, p. 28.
44. *Ibid.*,
45. S.N. Ganguly, *Tradition Modernity and Development : A Study in Contemporary Indian Society*, MacMillan of India, Delhi, 1977 p. 79.
46. See Ehsnul Haq., *op. cit.* p. 30.
47. With the result, some progress in education has taken place. There were 1,55,017 Primary Schools with 61,09,752 pupils in the year 1921-22, it rose to 19,244 primary schools with 1,02,24,288 pupils in the year 1936-37.
48. However, the scheme of basic education gradually lost its importance, because of its manual and mechanical nature of work, lack of

trained teachers, inadequate administration, absence of well planned programme and renewed interests in industrial development of free India, see Ehsnul Haq., *op. cit.*, p. 33.

49. S.K. Saini, *Development of Education in India. Socio-Economic and Political Perspective*, Cosmo Publications, New Delhi, 1980, p. 80.
50. *Ibid.*, p. 93.
51. J.P. Naik, *Policy and Performance in Indian Education 1947-74*, Dr. K.G. Saiyidain Memorial Trust, New Delhi, 1975, p. 3.
52. *Ibid.*
53. For details see *Report of the Secondary Education Commission*, (*1952-53*), Ministry of Education and Social Welfare, Government of India, New Delhi, 1972, pp. 36-37.
54. Report of Indian Education Commission (1964-66), *op. cit.*, 201.
38. *Ibid.*, p. 251.
56. R.K. Bhandari, Educational Development in the Seventh Five Year Plan, *New Frontiers in Education*, Vol. XIII, No. 4, October-December, 1983, p. 55.
57. *Ibid.*
58. *Ibid.*
59. S. Nural Hassan, *Challenges in Education, Cultural and Social Welfare*, Allied Publishers, New Delhi, 1977, p. 32.
60. R K. Bhandari, *op. cit.*, p. 60. This study reveals that the allocation of funds for education have been reduced from 5 per cent in first plan to 2.6 per cent in the sixth plan.
61. For details see J.C. Aggarwal, *National Policy on Education*, Arya Book Dept., New Delhi, 1979, and the *Gazetteer of India* Vol IV, Administration and Public Welfare, Ministry of Education and Social Welfare, Government of India, New Delhi, 1978, pp. 465-69.
62. For details of the Draft Policy see J.C. Aggarwal, *op. cit.*, pp. 465-69.
63. For details see *Challenge of Education—A Policy, Perspective*, Ministry of Education, Government of India, New Delhi, August, 1985.
64. For details see *National Policy on Education—1986*' Ministry of Human Resource Development, Government of India (Department of Education) New Delhi, May, 1986.
65. A.R. Kamat, The Educational Situation, *Economic and Political Weekly*, Vol. 7, No. 26, June, 1972, pp. 1229-1236.
66. *Ibid.*,
67. R.S. Tiwari, Adult Education Programme—Some Apprehensions, *Indian Journal of Adult Education*, October, 1978, p. 14.
68. Amiya Rao, Primary Education Problems and Purpose, *Economic and Political Weekly*, Vol. 25, No. 10 March 8, 1980, p. 503.
69. Karuna Ahmed, Towards and Study of Education and Social Change, *Economic and Political Weekly*, Vol. 14, No. 4 January, 27, 1979, p. 157.

70. *Ibid.*, p. 160.
71. J.P. Naik, *Policy and Performance in Indian Education 1947-74, op. cit*, p. 11.
72. Karuna Ahmed, *op. cit.*, p. 160.
73. A.R. Desai, *Social Change and Educational Policy*, in M.S. Gore and Others (ed.,) *Papers in the Sociology of Education in India*, NCERT., New Delhi, 1975, p. 119.
74. Karuna Ahmed, *op. cit.*, p. 161.
75. S.C. Bhatia, *Education and Socio-Cultural Disadvantages*, Xeroxes Publications, Delhi, 1982, p. 17.
76. *Ibid.*, pp. 17-18.
77. Sateswari Saxena, *op. cit.*, p. 2.
78. Bertrand Russel, *Education and the Social Order*, Unwin Paperbacks, London, 1977, p. 94.
79. J.P. Naik, *Elementary Education in India-A promise to keep*, Allied Publishers, New Delhi, 1975, p. 46. Also see the books by the same author, *Policy and Performance in Indian Education : 1947-74, op. cit.*, and *Equality, Quality aud Quantity—The Triangle in Indian Education*: Allied Publishers, New Delhi, 1975, for details.
80. See for details, J.P. Naik, *Elementary Education in India-A Promise to keep, op. cit.*, p. 46-57.
81. For details see, J.P. Naik, *Education in the Fourth Planning-Review and Perspective*, Nachiketa Publications, Bombay, 1968, pp. 17-26.
82. Iqbal Narain, *Rural Politics and Primary School Management*, in Rudolph and Rudolph (ed.,) *Education and Politics in India*, Studies in Organisation Society and Polity Harvard University Press, Cambridge, 1972, p. 148.
83. N.R. Inamdar, *Educational Administration in the Zilla Parishads in Maharashtra*, Popular Prakashan, Bombay, 1974, pp. 135-40.
84. See Iqbal Narain, K.C. Pande and Mohanlal Sarma, *Panchayati Raj and Educational Administration*, Aalikli Publishers, Jaipur, 1976.
85. Iqbal Narain, *Rural Politics and Primary School Management, op. cit.*, p. 152.
86. Report of Indian Education Commission 1964-66, *op. cit.*, p- 157
87. J.P. Naik, *Policy and Performance in Indian Education 1947-74, op. cit.*, p. 6.
88. In a survey conducted on 200 adult illiterates it was revealed that about 30 per cent of the respondents who learnt the letters and studied upto 3rd and 4th class during their childhood considered themselves illiterates, see G. Haragopal and G. Sudarshan, Rural Adult Literacy-An Enquiry into the Attitudes, *Indian Journal of Adult Education*, Vol. 47, October, 1978.
89. Raghunath Safaya, *Innovations and Latest Trends in Education*, The Associated Publishers, Ambala Contt., 1976, p. 130.

90. J.H. Oldhan, *Village Education in India : The Report of the Commission of Enquiry*, Oxford University Press, London, 1922.
91. A few among them are R.C. Das, *An Investigation into the Problems of Wastage and Stagnation at Primary Level of Education* (*Ph. D., thesis*) Gauhati University, 1970, L.R., Desai and K.G. Desai, *Wastage in Secondary Education in Gujarat*, A.G. Teachers College Ahemdabad, 1957, R.C. Sarma, *Wastage and Stagnation in Primary and Middle Schools in India*, NCERT, New Delhi, 1969 ; G.P. Tiwari, *Family Dynamics of Drop-out at the Primary Level* (*Ph. D., thesis*) Agra University, 1970, Goverment College of Education, Jabalpur, *A Study of Incidence and Causes of Wastage and Stagnation in Primary Schools of Madhya Pradesh*, 1973.
92. M. Kistaiah, K. Seetaram Rao and G. Sudarshan, Report of the study team on drop-outs at Primary School Level in Rural Areas (typed) submitted to *State Committee on Panchayati Raj Institutions*, Goverment of Andhra Pradesh, 1981.
93. J.P. Naik, *Some Perspective of Non-Formal Education*, *op. cit.*, p. 104.
94. N.R. Inamdar, *Educational Administration in the Zilla Parishads in Maharashtra*, *op. cit.*, pp. 136-137.
95. S. Rajgopal, *A critical Study of English Curriculum at the Primary and Secondary Stages of Education in the Madras State* (*Tamil Nadu*) Ph. D., thesis, Annamalai University, 1972 in M.B. Buch (ed.,) *A Survey of Research in Education*, Centre for Advanced Study in Education M.S. University, Baroda, 1974, p 295.
96. P.K. Bose, R.K. Banerjee and S.P. Mukherjee, *Educational Facilities Available in Higher Secondary School of West Bengal* (*1963-64*), Calcutta University, 1965, in M.B. Buch (ed.,) *Second Survey of Research in Education* Society for Educational Research and Development, Baroda, 1979, p. 464.
97. D.P. Tiwari, *Thoughts on Education*, Chugh Publications, Allahabad, 1972.

2

The Environment of Education

The efficiency of any system depends upon the environment in which it operates. As Riggs observed that the ecology of Public Administration is as much a limiting factor as is the ecology of biological species or cities.[1] The interaction between the environment and administration is very relevant at the grass-root level.[2] Thus, understanding of ecology of education in rural areas helps us to understand the functioning of educational system in these areas. Education is a sub-system of a major social, political and economic system. It is in this context, an attempt is made to examine the ecological framework of the district and the three villages selected for the purpose of the study. This attempt is made to give a detailed sketch of environment, the influence of which can be perceived throughout the study. It also helps in examining the impact of environmental factors on the working of the educational institutions.

The district Warangal selected for this study lies in the Telangana part of Andhra Pradesh, covering an area of 12,835 sq. kms. It is situated at a distance of 150 km. from Hyderabad —the State Capital. The density of population (Census

1971) was 145 persons per km. and the population of the district was 23.04 lakhs in 1981, of which the percentage of rural population was 86.6 and urban 13.4. The district consisted of three revenue division and fifteen talukas. There were 1,098 revenue villages in the district. There were fourteen Panchayat Samities which includes four ordinary, nine backward and one tribal blocks.[3]

Historical Context

The historical background of this district under study, in matters of education and culture, has been quite impressive. Hanamkonda which is a part of Warangal City was a famous centre of learning which distinguished it from the other parts from early times. This place, in its hey days, enjoyed fame and attracted scholars, some of whom thronged to its Jaina Basadis and Saivite monasteries. The tradition of learning was fostered by a succession of enlightened dynasties. From the Satavahnas down to the Kakatiya times there was an unbroken line of kings and conquerors who patronised learning.[4] The Muslim Dynasties like the Bahmanis, Qutub Shahis, Mughals and Asaf Jahis, which succeeded one another were patrons of Arabic, Persian and Urdu learning and, therefore helped to continue the intellectual tradition though not the indigenous learning.[5]

Concrete steps were taken for the introduction of modern education in the district alongwith the state only in the second half of the 19th Century A.D. The records indicate that two Persian and two 'Vernacular' schools were established which functioned in Hanamkonda and Matwada localities of Warangal[6] at that time.

The period between A.D. 1873 and A.D. 1882 was a period of expansion in the field of education. Public instruction became a major department by 1884 A.D. By that time, there was increasing demand for English education. With the result during 1880s, an anglo-vernacular school was established at Warangal. It soon developed into a high school by 1890-91. A few anglo-vernacular schools, which imparted Western education, were also started in the district. The establishment of the Osmania University in the year 1918 led to the establishment of Osmania high schools with Urdu as a medium of instruction in the state, leading to establishment of such schools in the districts also. Thus by 1926-27, the Government Middle School at Warangal was upgraded into an Osmania high school. This however, did not adversily affect the promotion of English education.[7]

Primary Education

From the later decades of the 19th Century, primary education became the sole responsibility of the government in the district. The *Jaghirdars* and Missionaries of both the Christian and non-Christian type also maintained some primary schools.[8] It was from the second decade of this century that the education in general and primary education in particular received greater attention. With the formation of Panchayat Samithis in 1959, the management of elementary education was transferred to them. As a result a large number of primary schools in the district were put under the control of the Panchayat Samithis. This is evident from the fact that out of 1,281 schools during 1967-68, as many as 1,209 were under the control by the Samithis.

Though a scheme of compulsory primary education was introduced in 1947, on an experimental measure in ten selected centres of which Warangal town was one, it could not make much progress for want of legal sanction to enforce regular attendance in the schools. Later the Andhra Pradesh Primary Education Act of 1961 was passed to cover the enrolment of all the children in the age-group of 6 to 11 within a period of five years. This was sought to be implemented by the local bodies within their respective territorial jurisdiction.

Another important aspect in the history of education has been the introduction of the system of Basic Education. Mahatma Gandhi advocated a child-centred system of education in which both teaching and learning should be organised through doing. He said that the craft which is suitable to the school and the physical environment of the child should be medium of instruction and that the selected craft should be correlated with the curriculum.[9]

The then Government of Hyderabad decided to implement the system of basic education and declared its policy of replacing the then existing system of general education by basic education in February, 1954. Methods adopted for spreading basic education were the establishment of basic training schools and conversion of a few conventional schools into basic schools. The growth of Basic Training Schools and basic schools till 1961, was very impressive. By the end of 1961-62 there were Six Teacher Training Schools and 58 Junior and 27 Senior basic schools. Thereafter, the basic education system underwent several organisational and curricular changes.

During the Second Five Year Plan period there was a retardation in the growth of basic schools. There was a change in the curriculum from its craft-centred nature to mere craft-orientation. By the year 1964-65 the number of Junior Basic Schools in the district came down to 36 and training schools to 5. The integrated curriculum was implemented by 1965-66 in all the seven classes of elementary sector. The Junior and Senior basic schools were replaced by primary and upper primary schools respectively.

Secondary Education

Till 1880s, no concrete measure was taken for introducing secondary education in the district either by government or or any other private agency. It was in 1880s, the erstwhile Nizam's Government established an Anglo-Vernacular school at the district headquarters which grew into a high school in the year 1890-91. Between 1885 and 1887, two more middle schools were opened in the town. By the end of the 19th Century, secondary education became the sole responsibility of the government in the district. The expansion of primary education during 1910s created pressure for expansion of secondary education. Secondary education naturally developed only from this period. With the result, the number of schools rose to 126 from a total number of 2 schools. The number of school going children increased from 392 to 55,955 by the year 1967-68.

Present Position

The position of education in the district at the time of study reveals that, this district was backward in terms of education level. The percentage of literacy in the district was 23.38 (1981). It was low when compared to 29.92% in Rayalaseema 32.78% in Coastal Andhra and to 26.62% in Telangana region.[10] The average state literacy was 29.94 per cent as per 1981 Census. The number of female literates was 1,60,000 and male literates was 3,90,000 in the district.

The district was provided with 1,462 primary schools (1981 Census) of which 990 were single-teacher schools. There were 40 model schools, 238 upper primary schools, and 196 secondary schools (high schools) in the district. There were about 20 Junior Colleges, 7 Degree Colleges in the district. There were two Polytechnics, one Government I.T.I., one College of Education, a Regional Engineering College, one Private Engineering College, one Ayurvedic College, one Oriental College, one Music and Dance School, and one Deaf and Dumb School. There was also a University in the district. In addition to these institutions 180 Non-formal Education, Centres, 300 Adult Education Centres were also in existence in the district. As per the IVth All India Educational Survey (updated data) 2,128 Habitations out of 2,395 habitations in this district were covered by primary schools. This covers 88.8% of the population. Distance-wise it works out to 1.5 km. radius with regard to upper primary schools covering 1,477 Habitations. This works out to 61.7% coverage of total habitations and 75.64% population. Distance-wise these schools were located within the radius of 3 kms.[11]

Social Setting

The district is primarily a unilingual district, as more than eighty per cent of the population speak Telugu. The principal religious groups are Hindus, Muslims and Christians consisting 93%, 5% and 2% respectively. Hindus are again subdivided into various castes. Caste plays an important role in the socio-political aspects of the society.

Reddys were socially, economically and politically a

powerful caste.[12] They command the district politics and economy. The politico-economic domination of Reddys stem from their grip over the means of production like land and capital. Though numerically few, the Brahmins still have considerable power base in the rural areas due to possession of land and Vathanas. Velamas who were similar to Reddys in economic position were the other powerful forward caste group. Vyshyas, another traditionally important caste, do not wield much influence in the rural areas. Most of them were engaged in petty business and money lending.

There were a number of backward castes in the district. They are Goudas, Gollas, Munnuru Kapu, Padmasali, Mudiraj Vadla, Kammari, Kummari, Ausula, Sakali, Mangali, Wad-dera, Besta. They together form a considerable proportion of the population in the district. Most of these castes were engaged either in agriculture or its allied activities.

Another most important caste group in terms of its numerical strength and political importance was Harijans.[13] Numerically Harijans were the single largest caste which accounts for 15.9 per cent of total population of the district. This is the caste which was most backward in all respects—social, economic, education and political. Most of them were still agricultural labourers and live outside the villages.

Apart from these castes, there were Scheduled Tribes, such as Lambadas, Koyas, Chenchus and Hill Reddys, who together accounted for 2.3 per cent of the total population of the district.

Economic Conditions

This District has been predominantly an agricultural district. There were no major irrigation sources. The agriculture mostly depends on monsoon. Important sources of irrigation were wells, rivulets, streams, lakes and tanks. Both food-grains and commercial crops were cultivated in the district. The important crops were Paddy, Millets, Pulses and Oil-Seeds. The principal occupation of a majority of the people continues to be agriculture. Others were engaged in industries, trade and commerce. A few were also engaged in caste occupations such as tailoring, weaving, washing the clothes, toddy tapping pottery etc. The total working population of the district (1981 Census) was 9,93,685. This constitutes 43.18 per cent of the total population in the district.

Further details about the occupational particulars of the district working population (1971 Census) reveal that agricultural labourers comprise 37.30%, cultivators 34.70%, 3.55% were engaged in livestock, forestry, fishing, hunting, planeterian, orchards and other allied activities, 0.04% in Mining and quarrying, 5.98% in household industry, 4.34% other than household industry, 1.16% construction, 3.88% in trade and commerce, 2.20% in transport, storage and communication and 0.70% other services.

In the district there were 47.0 per cent, 19.9 per cent, 16 6 per cent and 16 5 per cent of marginal, small, medium and big farmers respectively. The marginal, small, medium and big farmers own 8.4 per cent, 11.5 per cent, 18.8 per cent, and 61.3 per cent of the land respectively. This shows that the marginal and small farmers constitute 67 per cent and possess 20 per cent of the operated area while the medium and big farmers constitute 33 per cent and own 80 per cent of the operated areas.[14]

Political Situation

Political situation is also a major factor which influences the functioning of educational and other institutions in any area. This district has been one of the politically active districts in the Telangana region of the state.

The Congress-I and the Communist Parties (CPI, CPM and CPI-ML) have been the major political parties of the district and Bharatiya Janata Party was also striving to strike its roots. With the recent (1983) Assembly elections in the state, 'Telugu Desam' emerged as a significant political party in the district. But the Congress-I continues to be a dominant party in the district. It held seven out of thirteen Assembly seats and two Lok Sabha seats at the time of the study. Telugu Desam held four seats, BJP and CPM held one each of the Assembly seats. The Congress Party has its base in the Scheduled Castes, Scheduled Tribes and religious minorities (Muslims and

Christians), and being nurtured by upper middle class Reddy and Brahmin leaders. The Communist Parties are having their influence in certain parts of rural hinterland and in a segment of urban working class and student communities.

The Villages

For the purpose of micro analysis of the study three schools, viz., primary, upper primary and secondary schools were selected. They are located in Peta, Konda and Kur villages respectively.[15] This would facilitate an examination of the problems of all the types widely prevalent in rural areas. The village Peta was a single-teacher school for a long time. Another important factor weighed in selecting these schools has been the linkage in catering the educational needs of the children of these three villages. The Peta village pupil after completing their studies at the village go to Konda village for upper primary studies, and to Kur village school for secondary education.

These villages were situated at a distance of 13 km., 16 km. and 23 km. respectively from the district headquarters. While the Konda and Kur villages were well connected with a road from district headquarters leading to Mulug and Eturunagaram, the Peta village was situated about 2 km., away from the road. During the rainy season it was cut-off from the road as it was not connected with the main road and was surrounded by three 'vagus' (Streams) which delink the village from the other villages during the rainy season. People had to walk in knee-deep water and mud for two kms., to reach any of its surrounding villages. The school going children of this village were no exception to it.

The other two villages had access to the city. They also had facility of several R.T.C. Buses plying over the villages to the city very frequently. While the Konda and Kur villages were fullfledged Gram Panchayats having their own hamlets, the Peta was a hamlet of Konda village. Konda was having three hamlets attached to it. The village Kur was having two hamlets.

Peta was having a single-teacher school. Konda was having an upper primary school. There was also one successfully managed private primary school. Kur was having two separate schools working under two separate headmasters. One was upper primary school and another a high school (secondary school). It also had two private primary schools started recently. While Konda and Kur villages were having post office and telephone facilities, the Peta village had no such facilities, except a post-box hanged to a wall. Konda and Kur villages were having Veterinary hospital. The people of Peta had to depend upon the veterinary hospital at 'Konda'. None of these three villages were having the facility of a government hospital. The villagers had to depend on a few quacks who were staying in these villages. There were two MBBS doctors who opened their private clinics at Konda and Kur villages. Unlike the other two villages, Kur village was having a Branch of Canara Bank and a Branch Library of Zilla Granthayala Sanstha. A weekly market was also organised in the village on every Friday. People from surrounding villages carry their market transactions here.

Social Setting of the Villages

The Peta, Konda and Kur villages were having a population of about 500, 3000 and 6,500 respectively. The household particulars of the villages reveal that there were 105 households in the Peta village, 541 households in the Konda, 1220 households in Kur villages. The caste-wrae break-up of the households was as follows :

Caste-Wise Break-up of Households

Caste	Number of Households		
	Kur	Konda	Peta
Reddy	158 (12.95)	93 (17.19)	22 (20.95)
Vysya	6 (0.49)	10 (1.85)	—
Brahmins	11 (0.50)	5 (0.92)	—
Muslims	52 (4.26)	26 (4.80)	—
Telaga	152 (12.46)	14 (2.58)	—
Gouda	154 (12.62)	33 (6.10)	—
Mudiraj	200 (16.39)	44 (8.13)	30 (28.57)

Padmasali	92 (7.54)	32 (5.91)	33 (31.53)
Yadava	60 (4.92)	55 (10.16)	16 (15.29)
Chakali	72 (5.90)	30 (5.54)	3 (2.85)
Mangali	14 (1.15)	6 (1.11)	—
Vadla	16 (1.31)	10 (1.85)	—
Kummari	4 (0.32)	12 (2.22)	—
Kammari	9 (0.74)	3 (0.55)	—
Ousula	4 (0.32)	2 (0.36)	—
Aaremarati	—	32 (5.91)	—
Mera	1 (0 08)	7 (1.29)	—
Medari	3 (0.24)	3 (0.55)	—
Katika	7 (7.57)	3 (0.55)	—
Kanchari	1 (0.08)	1 (0.18)	—
Jangon	2 (0.16)	1 (0.18)	-
Batraju	2 (0.16)	—	—
Balija	—	1 (0.18)	—
Harijana (S.C.)	190(15.57)	114 (26.61)	—
Erukala (S.T.)	7 (0.57)	4 (0.74)	1 (0.95)
Total	1220	541	105

The above table explains that, there were about 23 Twentythree castes in Kur village, 24 Twentyfour castes in Konda village and six castes in Peta village. The Peta village was a small Hamlet of 105 households. It does not have the Scheduled Caste households. In all it had only six castes, of which the Scheduled Tribe family was a recent addition. This family came recently from the neighbouring village to eke out their livelihood in this village. Of the six castes of Peta village, Reddy caste was the socially and economically dominating caste. The Padmasali (Weaving) and Mudiraj (Fishery community) castes comprise a large porportion. The Golla (Shepherd community) Chakali (Washermen) and Erukala (Pig rearing community) families of the village were not only numerically thin, but socially, economically, educationally far behind the rest of the castes.

Of all the three villages, 'Kur' was the biggest village, having 1220 households. In this village, Reddy was the socially, economically, politically and educationally a dominant caste having considerable numerical strength. Mudiraj, Harijana,

Telagala (Farming community) and Gouda (Toddy tapping community) were the numerically dominating castes in the village. A few families of them were also socially, economically and politically in a dominating position. They own some land, have educational background and political experience. In this village each caste was an organised group. Most of them were having their caste 'Sangams' (Associations) i.e., Geeta Parisramika Sangam of Goudas, Munnurukapu Sangam of Telagala community, Matsya Karmika Sangam of Mudirajas etc. Chakali caste househods were also in considerable number. Harijans were also in a large number. The remaining castes mostly were service castes and were not sizeable in numbers, low in social status and poor in economic sphere.

The Konda village with 541 households was a medium size village. Reddys were large in number only next to the Harijans, They dominate social, economic and political scene. Though Mudiraj. Golla, Chakali families were large in number, they were socially, economically and politically very backward. Aaremarate—a migrated group from Maharashtra—and Gouda were also in considerable number and a few of them held high status in social, economical and political fields. The remaining were service castes like Kammari, Kummari, Vadla, Medari (Basket making community), Mera (Tailoring community), Ousula (Goldsmith). Mangali etc. They were very few in number and were backward in social, economic and political spheres. Harijans were the largest caste group in the village but the lowest in social, economic and political status. Erukulas, the only S.T. community in the village, eke their livelihood from pig rearing and mat making. Their social status, economic and educational level was lowest in the village.

In all the three villages, Forward Communities i.e., Reddys, Vyshyas, Brahmins and a few Muslim families constitute around 20 per cent of the total households. While there was no Scheduled Caste community in Peta village, they constitute 15 per cent and 26 per cent of the households of Kur and Konda villages respectively. In all the three villages Schedulѐd Tribes (Erukala caste, the only S.T. community of three villages) constitute less than one per cent of the total households. The remaining (nearly 70 to 80 percent) households belong to various castes of

Backward Community. This includes Mudiraj, Golla, Gouda, Telaga, Padmasali and other service castes like Kammari, Kummari, Medari, Chakali etc. The Forward Castes, Backward Castes and Scheduled Castes and Scheduled Tribes are the upper, middle and low castes of the society respectively.

The untouchability was not openly pract ced. However, Harijans receive a low level treatment on all occasions. Harijans still perform the traditional occupations like Chappal (Shoe) making and repairing. A large number of them were engaged as agricultural labourers.

Child marriage which adversely affect school education was still prevalent in these villages. In most of the Harijan and other backward castes, men at twenty and women at foruteen become parents. Most of the low caste and middle caste children were engaged as farm labourers and cattle rearers. A few low and middle caste children were engaged in beedi making activity in all the villages. Some of the middle caste women were also engaged in beedi making activity. Their kids assist them in rolling the leaves and filling them with tobacco powder.

These traditional occupations alongwith the child labour, beedi making etc., activities largely involve the children, which in turn affect their education.

Economic Pattern of the Villages

Agriculture was the main occupation and a source of livelihood for the people of the villages under study. Occupations of all the Reddys, Telagas has been cultivation. A large proportion of the people from the Vyshyas rely on agriculture. other castes depended on agriculture and business. A few landed Muslim families were also living on agriculture, and Other Muslim families were engaged in petty trading, daily wages and certain jobs like lorry drivers, cleaners etc. The Gouda Community in these villages generally live on their traditional toddy tapping and some of them were also engaged in agriculture. Though most of the Mudiraj households resort to their traditional occupation of fishing, they get this work only for a few months in a year. For the rest of the year, they eke out their living by selling seasonal fruits like seetaphal, mangoes, bananas, etc. A few live by selling ice-cream and sodas at bus stops and in the village streets. During the period of agricultural operations, they work as farm labourers (men and women). Very few Mudirajas who have a piece of land live on their own agriculture. 'Padmasali' (Weavers) community in all these villages live on their traditional occupation of weaving and a few of them perform petty cloth trading, tailoring etc. A few Padmasalis eke out their living by selling cloth by moving from village to village and also in weekly markets. Padmasali women and children help their men in weaving activities, work as farm labourers and beedi-makers for most of the year.

'Yadavs' (Golla) mostly live on their traditional occupation i.e., sheep rearing. A considerable number of them work as farm labourers and 'Jeetagallu' (contracted labour for a year). Their women mostly live on farm labour and other daily wage works. Except few who live on agriculture, all the 'Chakali' and 'Mangali' households live on their traditional occupations viz., washing clothes and hair cutting respectively. Their women in most of the case work as farm labourers. 'Vadla', 'Kummari' and 'Kammari' families live on their traditional occupations i.e., Carpentary, Pottery and Blacksmithy respectively. 'Ausula', 'Kanchari' and 'Mera' families live on their age-old occupations as Goldsmith, Aluminium works and tailoring respectively. While 'Jangam' being a type of 'Poojari' community (a sect of shaivites) live on agriculture, performing ritual ceremonies and a few as patwaris (Village accountant). 'Katika' caste people live on their traditional meat selling business and other labour activity.

Harijans mostly live as daily wage labourers, farm labourers and 'Jitagallu'. In summer season when agricultural work is not available they dig wells, level the lands on daily wage basis as well as on contract basis. Side by side they also perform their traditional leather work. Harijan women and children mostly work as daily labourers in farms and other activities. The 'Erukala' families live on their sweat and toil by pig rearing and working as daily labourers.

In these activities, except a few who have substantial land and income, all others press their children into service to eke out the livelihood. The poor families also employ their children as contract labourers (Jeetam) or daily labourers at the tender ages to supplement their family income. All these factors have a direct bearing on the educational development of the villages.

Land being an important source of income in rural areas, there is a possibility of those who have substantial land, sending their children to school in more numbers. An examination of the land ownership pattern in 'Peta' village shows that, out of total 105 households, 10 families held more than ten (but not more than 15) acres of land each. About 18 households own 5 to 10 acres of land, about 72 families held below 5 acres of land and there are only five families who did not possess any land. In 'Konda' village, out of total 541 households about 30 households owned 10 and more acres. About 60 families held 5 to 10 acres and about 275 households belonged to below 5 acres category. In this village 176 families were landless. In 'Kur' village there were about 1220 households, of which 50 families were in possession of 10 and above acres of land, a few of them owned more than 40 acres. About 170 households owned 5 to 10 acres, about 500 families belonged to below 5 acres category. Another 500 families of this village were landless. The households who own 10 acres and above were from forward castes, mostly Reddys. The families who owned 5 to 10 acres of land also mostly belonged to forward castes and other middle caste, like Telaga, Gouda and Aaremarati. Those who owned below 5 acres of land were mostly backward castes like Golla, Mudiraj, Chakali, Kammari, etc., and few Harijans. The landless poor mostly belong to the Scheduled Castes and the Scheduled Tribes and a few service castes like Chakali, Medari, Mangali, etc. By and large, in these villages, larger landholdings were in the hands of Upper Castes and the smaller land holdings were in the hands of Backward Castes and the landless were the people who belong to the Scheduled Castes.

Political Pattern of the Villages

During the period of study all these villages under study were in the grip of Bharatiya Janata Party. In the Assembly elections (January 1982) a majority of the people in these villages voted to the BJP candidate, who won the elections from this constituency defeating a Congress-I candidate. The Telugu Desam wave did not touch these villages. Earlier these villages supported the Congress Party. But, in the last two general elections to the State Assembly, a majority were supporting the BJP candidate, who maintains cordial relation with newly emerging upper and backward caste leaders of the villages. At the time of the study there were only two parties in the villages-one was BJP and another was Congress-I

The impact of politics on school education could not be perceived in 'Peta' village, as it happens to be a small village. In 'Konda' village, though the Congress-I and BJP worked against each other, they did not touch the school affairs. Whereas in 'Kur' village the two parties successfully worked against teachers' efforts to construct a school building and getting the sanction of a hospital. In this process of one working against another, they could not construct the school building though it is sanctioned, and they could not get the hospital approved.

Educational Setting of the Villages

Educational setting in all the three selected villages was not conducive for attaining its objectives. 'Peta' village had a single-teacher Primary School, run under the Panchayati Samithi. This school was opened on 2-7-1956 under the development programme 1956-57. Earlier very few people who were interested in their children's education were either sending their children to a nearby school or engaged a teacher privately. The first teacher who was appointed in 1956 was transferred within a period of one month. Mr. K.L. was posted as teacher. He stayed for nearly two years (August 1956 to January 1958) and took some interest in development of the school. During this period three classes were started and about thirty pupils were attending the school. After him another teacher Mr. B.S. joined the school. He was native of a nearby village ($3\frac{1}{2}$ km). Then young in age, he evinced considerable interest in maintaining discipline and also expansion of the school. He opened new classes upto 5th and managed all the classes single handedly as he was a teacher with commitment. His period is still remembered by the village people as the best period in school education.

Soon after the transfer of Mr. B.S. Mr. K.V. was posted. Mr. K.V. worked for about eight years (August 1963 to November 1971). In the initial stages, he also strived to maintain the standards that his predecessor set. But when he went on for training programme for about one and half years, Mr. M.K. was posted in the leave vacancy on a temporary basis. The new teacher could not cope up with the strength and gradually closed down certain sections, Mr. K.V. returned from training in April 1967 and worked till December 1971. After his return from training he also did not evince interest. The children studying V class had to go to neighbouring villages for their education. They had to walk about 7 kms daily for their primary, middle and high school education. Thus the expansion and education suffered a great deal due to the indifference of the subsequent teachers.

After the transfer of Mr. K.V. another teacher Mr. C.R.C. was posted. This teacher by then crossed 50 years. He was coming to the school from the district headquarters (Warangal, 15 kms) daily. He used to travel by bus every day. He worked in the village till his retirement on 11th May, 1977 (about six years). His period was virtually a period of decay in the school education. He did not take any interest in the school education because of his old age and domestic problems. Although the village elite took some interest and pressurised the teacher for retaining the higher classes, they lost the interest in the school. This was partly due to the fact that the children of some of the elite crossed the stage of primary education and they did not need the expansion any more.

After retirement of Mr. C.R.C. (11-5-1977), no teacher was posted for nearly six months. The school was virtually closed as it was a single teacher school. It is in the October, 1977, Mr. G.S.R. joined the school. He worked for nearly seven years. At the time of the study, the school almost got stagnated. Nobody bothered about the school. The newly emerging elite of the village put their children in the schools at Warangal town. A few families sent their children to neighbouring village. The school had nothing except a few yards of open place. The little thatched hut no longer existed due to the negligence of villagers and teacher.

The analysis of the historical aspect of the 'Peta' village shows that, the development of a school, apart from other things, mostly depends on the interest shown by the teacher. This analysis also shows how the education suffers in a single-teacher school, when the teacher is not interested in the job. Still, two-thirds of the total children in the school-going-age (6-18) were illiterate and were outside the school system.

The history and environment of education of 'Konda' village reveals that the village school was established in the year 1920-21 as a single-teacher school. Later it became central primary school and recently upgraded into an upper primary school. In the initial stages there were only 15 boys. By the year 1930 the strength of the school rose to 60 and classes were run up to IV. The medium of instruction was Urdu, mostly attended by forward caste children. This includes Reddys, Brahmins, Muslims. No Harijan child was attending the school at that time. By the year 1930, the number of teachers was raised to two. By the year 1950, the strength of the school rose to 140, the number of teachers was three. It rose to 4 by 1958. The school did not have a building of its own till June, 1966. Classes were run in two separate rented houses. While the rent for one house was being paid by the government, the rent for the other house was paid from the contribution of villagers. Lack of co-operation and unity among the people and lack of interest on the part of the village elite hampered educational development. According to a leader from a backward caste, the village elite were jealous of the backward class families sending their children to the school.

However, a two-room building was constructed in the year 1967 and was inaugurated by the then collector of the district. The classes were added upto 5th. The strength of the school was about 150. With a few changes the same conditions and facilities obtained during the last seventeen years. It is only recently (at the time of the study) another room was added. Though Class-VI was introduced during 1982-83 to make it a middle school, there was no improvement in the school building nor in the total strength of teaching staff. One room constructed for the purpose of Gram Panchayat was being used by the school. Yet half of the classes were conducted under the trees.

Though in reality there was only one school in 'Konda' village, there were three schools on paper. This includes Upper Primary School, one Girls Primary School and a Harijanwada Primary School. The Girls Primary School and Harijanwada Primary School had only one class. In practice they were merged with class-I of Upper Primary School. Teachers maintained three separate attendance registers for the class-I of these three different schools. The teacher who was going to class-I had to carry with him three registers to mark the attendance of children. The strength of all the three schools was 330 at the time of the study (1982-83).

There was also a private school successfully run by a Brahmin family (wife and husband). The children of forward and a few backward caste families not only of this village but even of adjacent villages were going to this school. There were about 60-70 pupils in this school studying class-I to class-V. The unimpressive performance of the Government School accounts for the genesis of this school. It strives in contrast with the government school.

The history and environment of this Konda school presents a different picture. It suffered right from the beginning due to vested interest. It also reveals the difficulties of an understaffed school where the classes often go without teaching. It also presents the difficulties of new schools which have no building and no equipment. The fact that about half of the children (6-18) were not in the school system is a sad comment on rural education.

The third village-the Kur selected for this study has its own history and environmental context. This village was under the dominion of erstwhile Hyderabad State. A Desai (Landlord) of 'Kur' village, was virtually the ruler in the area during the Nizam's rule. A big 'Gadi' (fort) in the village stands as testimony to his earlier dominance and repressive rule. Such a situation cannot provide the necessary atmosphere for furtherance of education. Most of the villagers recall that all the Harijan families were almost the bonded labourers of Desai. The Kapu (farming) families were to freely plough his lands. All the service castes like Chakali, Mangali, Vadla etc., were to do his work freely. No education was encouraged during these days. The situation, however, did undergo a change. One Chakali (Washerman) remarked", during Desai's period no child from Chakali community had ever attended the school." Children were physically dragged out of the school to attend to the works of Desai's home, same was the condition with Harijans.

There are no records available in the school to trace the history and evolution of the school. Therefore, the data was to be collected through informal and oral interviews. These discussions indicate that the government school existed prior to 1920. In the early days there were two primary schools : Girls Primary School and a Boys Primary School. Boys school had 5 teachers and girls school had 4 teachers. Till 1948 education was available upto V-class. A school for Harijan boys was also started but was merged later with Boys Primary School.

By the year 1957-58 the Boys Primary School got upgraded into a middle school with a facility to study upto VII class. In the year 1959-60 it became a high school and was renamed as Zilla Parishad Secondary School.

In the 'Kur' village also, in addition to one Secondary School and one Upper Primary School, there were two Private Primary Schools established recently (1982-83). The schools enrolled nearly 150 students each. There was still competition between these school to attract more number of students. One school had to reduce its monthly fee per student to attract poor students (one school was charging Rs. 10 per child per month and another was charging Rs. 5 per child per month). People prefer to send their children to these school instead of sending them to government school. For the poor Harijan parents, whose children get some assistance in the form of money and books in the government school, there was no alternative except to send their children to government schools.

Inspite of all these educational institutions in the village, still there were about 618 illiterate children of school going age (6-18) in the village at the time of the study. Of which 383 were girls and 235 were boys. Apart from illiterates there were about 113 drop-outs in 6-18 years age group. Of them 42 are girls and 71 boys. The school-going children (6-18 age) of the village account for 934 of which 660 were boys and 274 were girls.[16]

The study of 'Kur' village, shows that, in the beginning the masses suffered the oppression of Desai and kept their children out of the school. In the later period nobody took interest in building a good school. The existing schools were badly accommodated and ill-equipped which render them ineffective giving rise to private schools.

Summing-Up

The analysis of the environment of education in the district as well as in the villages selected for the study shows that the environment is not conducive for spreading and advancement of education. Though the district has had educational schemes in the pre-independence days, it lags behind in educational development compared to the regions and the state. Since the economic means and political institutions were in the hands of the upper caste people, the Scheduled Castes and backward class caste people do not have access to education. Majority of the schools in the district as well as all the schools of the villages selected for the study suffer from lack of accommoda-tion, physical equipment, learning materials etc. A majority of the teachers do not stay in the villages where they are working. The village elite do not evince much interest in the educational development of the villages. Most of them have put their children in the schools in Warangal town. The inefficiency of the government schools in providing proper education to the children was giving rise to private schools in the villages. The poor children cannot attend these schools. Historically also the villages remained backward in education due to the vested interests. The governments also continue to be indifferent towards the rural education. Since the masses are poor and struggling for their livelihood, they cannot take interest in educational matters of the village. Hence the environment in rural areas is not conducive for the development of education and to achieve the constitutional obligation of universalization of elementary education.

The study also indicates that about fifty per cent of the children of school going age were getting enrolled in the schools. The rest of the children have never seen the face of the school. This itself is an evidence which shows how far is the present rural education system to its goals.

REFERENCES

1. Fred W. Riggs, *An Ecological Approach : The Sala Model*, in Ferrel Heady and Sybl L. Stokes, *Papers on Comparative Public Administration*, Institute of Public Administration, University o Michigan, Ann Arbor, Michigan, 1961, p. 19.
2. G. Haragopal, *Administrative Leadership and Rural Development in India*, Light & Life Publishers, New Delhi, 1980, p. 51.
3. Taluks and Samithis were replaced by fifty Revenue and Panchay at Mandals during the Telugu Desam Party's rule in the State.
4. *Andhra Pradesh District Gazetteers, Warangal, op. cit.*, p. 170.
5. *Ibid.*
6. *Ibid.*, p. 171.
7. *Ibid.*
8. *Ibid.*, p. 173.
9. *Ibid.*, pp. 175-176.
10. Assistant Director (Plg. & Sts.) ; *Warangal District Plan 1980-85 Draft*, Warangal, p. 168.
11. *Ibid*, p. 169.
12. D. Ravindra Prasad, *Co-operatives and Rural Development: A Study of District Co-operative Central Bank in A.P.* : Osmania University, Hyderabad, 1978, p. 12 See Also Carolyn M. Elliott, Caste and Faction among the Dominant Caste : The Reddys and Kammas of A.P. in Rajni Kothari (Ed.,) *Caste in Indian Politics*, Orient Longman New Delhi, 1970, p. 129-171.
13. G. Sreenivas Reddy, *Administratian of Harijān Welfare Programmes—Case Study of a District of A P.*, Ph. D., Thesis, Department of Public Administration, Kakatiya University, 1981, p. 180.

14. Ch. Balaramulu, *Organisation and Working of a Small Farmers Development Agency—Case Study* (*Ph. D., Thesis*) Department of Public Administration, Kakatiya University, Warangal, 1980, p. 41.
15. Pseudonym.
16. These figures were collected through a door to door survey of the village.

3

Administrative Set-Up

A proper understanding of the educational system and its role in development of the nation calls for an analysis of the administrative set-up. This would provide scope to understand how education is being managed, and enable us in proper analysis of various issues involved in the system. The echo of the success or failure of the administrative machinery can be seen at the grassroot level.

Hence this chapter is devoted to a discussion on administrative set-up for education in the state of Andhra Pradesh with an emphasis on grassroots administration. A brief account of historical background is also given in this chapter. In the field level administration the major activities relating to personnel, finance and academic are discussed in detail. In addition, an attempt is made to examine the adequacy of physical equipment such as accommodation, furniture, sanitation, drinking water, teaching staff and welfare activities. Major focus of the chapter is on the policy of government for universalization of education, formation of certain skills and bringing about social awareness and social change through education. It is also examined whether the administrative set-up for education is suitable to the tasks set for education.

I. Historical Background

The management of educational administration in India during the pre-Independence period was under the British administration and the princely states. After Independence, the Department of Education in the Government of India was re-organised and a separate Ministry of Education was created. Efforts were made to unify and co-ordinate the official machinery for the administration of education in all the states without basically changing the then set-up. Re-organisation of states in 1956, necessitated certain adjustments in the administrative set-up for education.

The educational administration in the State of Andhra Pradesh has its own distinct history. The present system of educational administration emerged from different patterns that prevailed in the Nizam's Dominion and the Andhra region before, 1947.

In the Nizam's Dominion the Department of Education was responsible for all the educational matters in the State. There was one Education Secretary at the Secretariat level and Director of Public Instruction and other Sub-ordinate Officers at the executive level. The district level administration was looked after by the District Educational Officer, Deputy Inspectors and Inspectoresses. The Revenue District was coterminous with educational district.

The Andhra region had a different pattern, since it was under the composite State of Madras. The Department was headed by a Secretary in the Secretariat who was responsible for policy formulation. There was a Director of Public Instruction and a number of Regional Directors for implementation of policies. At the district level there were District Educational Officers and Inspectors working under them. The education district was not always coterminous with the revenue district.

After 1956, with the emergence of Andhra Pradesh, a Department of Education was created at the Secretariat level. All levels of education—primary, secondary, higher and technical—came under the purview of this Department. The Education Department is headed by a Secretary. He is assisted by Deputy Secretaries and Assistant Secretaries. The Secretariat was responsible for evolving general policies and plans and is expected to provide the liaison between Minister and various Directorates.

The Directorate was the executive body charged with the responsibility to implement the policies and plans. It was made responsible for organisation, inspection, supervision and maintenance of discipline. At the top level there was Director of Public Instruction, assisted by Deputy Directors, Assistant Directors and other personnel. The pattern at the regional and district levels remained intact.

After the introduction of Panchayati Raj in the year 1959, all the primary and secondary schools in the rural areas came under the control of the Panchayati Raj bodies. A post of Deputy Secretary (Education) was created at the Zilla Parishad level to look after the administration of schools managed by Zilla Parishad. Extension Officers for Education were appointed at the Samithi level for the management of schools at the grassroots level.

In the year 1965, some more changes were introduced in the Educational administration at the state as well as the district level. The monolithic character of the Director of Public Instruction was brought to an end. It was bifurcated into the Director of Public Instruction and the Director of Higher Education. The Colleges of Arts and Sciences, Physical Education, Oriental and Training Colleges were placed under the Director of Higher Education.

In the same year changes were also introduced at the district level in order to conform to the jurisdiction of block and revenue districts for purpose of planning and development. The posts of Regional Deputy Directors of Public Instruction were abolished. And the posts of District Educational Officers were elevated to the status of Deputy Director of Public Instruction and were made responsible for all educational matters in their respective districts.

The educational district was coterminous with the revenue district. The posts of Gazetted Inspectors of Schools were created under the overall supervision of District Educational

Officer to facilitate the inspection of Secondary and Training Schools in the districts.

Some changes were also made at the block level. The posts of the Deputy Inspectors of Schools were created at the headquarters of all the blocks to look after the academic inspection of the schools. They were completely independent of Panchayat Samithis and were accountable only to the District Educational Officer. Junior Deputy Inspectors of Schools were posted to assist the Deputy Inspectors of Schools at the block level.

A few changes were made at the headquarters in 1967. The Director of Public Instruction and the Director of Higher Education were merged as the bifurcation did not yield worthwhile results.

In the year 1975, the Directorate of Public Instructions was again bifurcated into the Directorate of Higher Education and the Directorate of School Education. A post of Additional Director for Primary Education was also created due to the tremendous increase in the number of Primary Schools, Secondary Schools and Higher Education. But the organizational structure at the district and block level that was devised in 1965 did not undergo any change.

One can see from the above account that while education rapidly expanded at all the levels, the changes in the structures were quite superficial. Changes mainly revolved around only structures. This type of bifurcation, unification and re-bifurcation of higher levels can make only a marginal difference to the entire educational administration.

II. Present Set-Up

In the existing administrative set-up (at the time of the study), at the apex of the educational administration, there is a Secretary for Education under a Minister who was responsible for policy and planning in education. On the executive side, there were two Directors viz,, the Director of Higher Education, who looks after the needs of the Higher Educational Institutions like Degree Colleges, Training Colleges etc., and the Director of School Education, who was incharge of Primary and Secondary Schools. Below the Director of School

Education there was one Additional Director for Primary Education. In addition to these two Directors, there was also a Director of Adult Education, to look after the National Adult Education Programme, being implemented from 1978 onwards.

Though till recently there was no intermediary level functionary between district and state level administration, in the year 1982, the posts of Regional Joint Directors of Higher Education, and the Regional Joint Directors of School Education were created at the regional level. This was done to facilitate and speed-up the educational operations. There were four such Regional Joint Directors of Higher Education in the state. One Joint Director's Office was located at the headquarters of Warangal District. The area of operation of this Regional Joint Director extends to nine districts of Telangana area, excluding the twin cities which are looked after by the Director of Higher Education himself.[1]

All those functions hitherto performed by District Educational Officers were now being performed by the Regional Joint Director of Higher Education. This includes all matters pertaining to the service conditions of Junior Lecturers working in Government Junior and Degree Colleges including the power of temporary appointment, transfers and discipline. This also covers the service matters relating to Physical Directors and Librarians in the Government Junior Colleges. The jurisdiction of these functionaries extend to the appeals pertaining to serve matters of non-teaching staff below the category of UDCs., working in Government Degree and Junior Colleges located in their respective jurisdiction. All correspondence from the Government Junior Colleges to the Directorate should be routed through the Regional Joint Director of Higher Education.

Regarding the Regional Joint Directorates of School Education, there were five such Directorates in the state, of which one was located at the headquarters of the district under study.[2] The jurisdiction of this Regional Joint Director of School Education extends to four districts of Telangana. The Regional Joint Director of School Education was assisted by two Assistant Directors and other office staff.

The main functions of the Regional Joint Director of School Education were : inspection of all the offices of District Educational Offices and Parishad Educational Offices under his jurisdiction ; granting of permission and recognition to English Medium Primary and Upper Primary Schools; appointments, promotions and transfers of Deputy Inspectors of Schools of Grade-I, School Assistants of Grade-I, Extension Officers (Education) Grade-I, and all non-gazetted Ministerial Staff (Superintendents, Auditors). This also includes granting permission to open higher classes including IX and X in English Medium and all the other types of schools. Recognition of all aided secondary schools ; budgeting, controlling and accounting for government grants and budgeting of district in the zone —Primary and Secondary Education ; Administering grant-in-aid relating to buildings, equipment, furniture, library etc., of Primary, Upper Primary Schools and Secondary Schools. All managements also fall under his jurisdiction. All appeals relating to primary school teachers under all managements ; first appeal in respect of all types of teachers under local bodies and appeals (Under Act 11/75) relating to aided Primary and Secondary Teachers have to be made to this functionary.

All these functions of the Regional Joint Director of Schools were only on paper. In reality it could not reduce the burden of the District Educational Officer. The Regional Joint Directorate was not in a position to perform all these functions as it was under-staffed and ill-equipped. The officials in the Regional Joint Directorate feel that they were only performing post-office duties i.e., routing the applications and files to the directorate.

At the district Level, the District Educational Officer was the overall incharge of educational administration. He looks into the matters of Primary and Secondary Education, including Junior Colleges. On the administrative side he was assisted by a Gazetted Administrative Officer. This post has been recently created to relieve the District Education Officer, from the routine matters like sanctioning of leave to Ministerial Staff, approval of routing drafts, maintenance of discipline of the office staff. On the academic side the District Educational Officer was assisted by Deputy Educational Officers, who were earlier known as Gazetted Inspectors, to look after Secondary Schools of private, government and local Bodies. There was one Parishad Educational Officer at Zilla Parishad,[3] who was earlier known as Deputy Secretary Education, to look after the administrative matters of all the Zilla Parishad Secondary Schools. He works under the administrative control of District Development Officer in the Zilla Parishad, who was previously designated as Secretary, Zilla Parishad and latter as Deputy Chief Executive Officer of the Zilla Parishad.

At the block level, there was a Deputy Inspector of Schools to look after academic inspection of the Primary and Upper Primary Schools under private, the government and the local bodies in the block area, where the number of schools under them is large, they were assisted by Junior Deputy Inspectors. In addition there was one Extension Officer (Education) in the Samithi, who was incharge of administrative matters of Primary and Upper Primary Schools in the block area. He works under the administrative control of Block Development Officer.[4]

The above presentation shows that the creation of an additional level only adds to the expansion of the existing system. This does not strengthen the grassroots system which has to tackle the problem. While the policy was to universalise education, the creation of additional posts at middle level was not an adequate and proper response to the problem. Moreover, the handing over of administrative matters of rural schools to Panchayati Raj created dual control over educational institution i.e., academic control by Panchayati Raj bodies. This creation of middle levels without proper equipment and dual control over rural school created a situation of lack of integration among various levels of educational administration.

III. Field Organization—Internal Structure

The District Educational Officer is incharge of field administration. He is of the rank of the Deputy Director in the state government. Although there were Joint Directors at regional level, the D.E.O's office has been an important link between the schools and managements on the one hand, Directorate and field administration on the other. District Educational Officer has to work in collaboration with other government officers at the district level, specially the officers of Zilla Parishad and Panchayat Samithi. With regard to academic matters the District Educational Officer has to inspect all the Junior Colleges and Teacher Training Institutes in the district. His other duties include inspecting Secondary Schools, having gazetted headmasters making visits to Secondary Schools, Upper Primary Schools, Primary Schools, Non-formal Education Centres, Adult Education Centres, Schools of Music and Dance, Oriental Schools, Night Primary Schools etc.[5] He has authority to review inspection reports of Deputy Educational Officers, and academic performance of teachers. He has to convene monthly meetings of Deputy Educational Officers, Parishad Educational Officers and the meetings of Deputy Inspectors of Schools and Extension Officers (Education) whenever necessary. He has to publish bulletins highlighting the academic advancement in the district, and perform several other functions which can improve the quality of education in the district.

District Educational Officer was empowered to constitute District Common Examination Board and take care of exmination for classes other than VII and X. He has to take advance action for the conduct of VII class common examination and X class public examination like setting the centres, appointment of departmental officers, custodians of question papers etc., and conduct the above examinations with the necessary care and caution. He has to organise spot valuation of answer scripts of these examinations. the tabulation and declaration of results. He has to issue the certificates for VII class common examination.

The various functions mentioned above shows that the District Educational Officer is over—burdened with a number of functions, for which it is physically impossible for him to do justice to these aspects.

To assist the District Educational Officer in administrative matters, recently, a post of gazetted Administrative Officer to D.E.O. was created in the D.E.Os Office. He has to perform the duties such as sanctioning of C.Ls to Ministerial Staff and Class IV employees, headmasters of Secondary School (non-gazetted) and Deputy Inspectors of Schools. He was also responsible for general supervision and maintenance of discipline in the case of Ministerial Staff and Class IV employees ; approving the routine drafts : and sanctioning of increments to all teaching and non-teaching non-gazetted staff.

There were four Deputy Educational Officers in the district to assist the District Educational Officer in academic matters. While one was attached to the D.E.Os Office, the others were posted in different places of the district, to be nearer to the rural schools. They have to conduct annual inspection of the Secondary Schools in the district and report to the D.E.O. They have to make follow-up visits to Secondary Schools, inspect 5% Upper Primary Schools in a year.

Since all the Primary and Secondary schools in the rural areas in the state have been brought under the control of the Panchayat Samithis and Zilla Parishads respectively, a standing committee for Education was created in the Zilla Parishad.[6] This committee has to look after all the matters of education like salaries of teachers, providing material to schools etc. The members of Zilla Parishad elect the members of the committee from among themselves.

The Education Wing at the Zilla Parishad level is headed by the Parishad Educational Officer. His responsibilities were, to look after the day-to-day administration of Zilla Parishad Secondary Schools and provide liaison between the Zilla Parishad and the Education Department. The Parishad Educational Officer has to work under the control of District Development Officer and the Chairman of Zilla Parishad. His main functions include; ensuring effective and timely follow-up action on the inspection reports of Zill Parishad Secondary Schools; visiting Zill Parishad Secondary Schools ; making surprise visits to Zill Parishad Secondary Schools and Samithi Primary and Upper Primary Schools ; reviewing examination results in Zill Parishad Secondary Schools ; ensuring implementation of the policies and programmes of the department in Panchayati Raj institutions, providing staff in Zill Parishad Secondary Schools as per the requirements; maintaining service registers of staff of

Secondary Schools and sanctioning of leave, increment etc. His other functions include forwarding applications for permission to open new classes and recognition of education institutions, assisting the D.E.O. in conducting various examinations and conference of Headmasters of Zill Parishad Secondary Schools on administrative and academic issues every year.

Parishad Educational Officer has to prepare budget estimates and submit them to D.E.O. He has to make arrangements for payment of salaries to Zilla Parishad School teachers and ensure proper utilization of educational grants.

While Zilla Parishad has been a responsible body for secondary education in rural areas, the Panchayat Samithi[7] was responsible for maintenance and expansion of primary and upper primary education. It was made responsible for improvement of accommodation and other facilities for schools and with people's participation. It was also responsible for taking of such action which may be necessary for the promotion of education of all the children until they complete the age of fourteen.

To fulfil these functions, the Samithis were having standing Committee for Education. As in the case of Zilla Parishad, the members of the Committee were elected by members of Samithi, and the Chairman of the Committee as per 1976 Amendment was to be elected from among the members of the Standing Committee.[8]

Academic matters of rural Primary and Upper Primary Schools were looked after by the Deputy Inspector of Schools, posted at the block headquarters. In urban areas both academic as well as administrative matters of Upper Primary and Primary Schools were looked after by Deputy Inspector of Schools. In areas the administrative matters of Upper Primary and Primary Schools are to be looked after by Extension Officer (Education). The functions of Deputy Inspectors of Schools include ; conducting annual inspection of Upper Primary Schools, Primary Schools and Night Primary Schools and submission of inspection reports ; making follow-up visits to these schools and making two surprising visits (a year) to the schools. He has to give demonstration lessons in the schools, and assess schools on the basis of their performance in curricular and extra curricular activities. He has to visit mid-day meals centres, and assist the D.E.O. in proper distribution of Nationalised Text Books. He has to scrutinise applications for recognition and grant-in-aid in respect of non-government schools and requests for adhoc grants. He has to collect educational statistics, conduct enquiries. and submit necessary statements for release of teaching and other grants to Primary Schools.

Wherever there are more number of schools under the Deputy Inspector of Schools, he was assisted by a Junior Deputy Inspector of Schools. The Junior Deputy Inspectors of Schools have to conduct annual inspection and follow-up visits, surprise visits to the Primary Schools and Night Primary Schools. They also assit the schools in improving their standards, and undertake supply of text books.

In the Panchayat Samithi there is an Extension Officer (Education) who works under the administrative control of Block Development Officer and the President of Panchayat Samithi. He has to look after the day-to-day administrative matters of the Panchayat Samithi Schools. He has to undertake inspection and supervision of Samithi Primary and Upper Primary Schools assigned by the D.E.O. and submit the reports. He has to inspect and visit hostels and schools in the Samithi area. Further he has to ensure improvement of enrolment and attendance of pupils of school age.[9]

At the village level the village panchayat has no specific role to play in educational administration. Every Gram Panchayat has to constitute functional committees for agriculture, public health and sanitation, and communication. If necessary it can constitute other committees like Committee for Education and Taxation.[10] Every school was having its own parents committee, (or school improvement committee) involving some villagers to look after certain problems like accommodation, teaching facilities etc., of the school. But these parent committees generally remain only on paper. They do not undertake any constructive activity. The parents committees generally include the leading village elite, whose children are generally admitted in the schools located in the town and cities.

At the grassroots level there was no democratic institution at the village where the actual implementation of universalization of education has to take shape. Though at Zilla Parishad and Samithi levels the popular bodies have been entrusted with some responsibilities, they have not been given the specific responsibility. On the administrative side they were not given full authority. Some powers are retained at the D.E.Os level. There was no proper method to integrate the activities of various levels and different agencies. Such an arrangement results in poor attention, weak supervision and ineffective implementation of the tasks at the village level.

IV. Activities at the Field Level Administration

The major activities of the field level educational administration can broadly be categorised into four groups viz., one Personnel, two ; Financial, three ; Academic and four ; Other activities,

1. Personnel

The important personnel matters of educational administration at the field level can be further categorised into six types. They are selection and placement, salary, administration, promotions, transfers, pension and provident fund and grievance machinery.

A. Selection and Placement

The District Educational Officer deals with all personnel matters of teachers of the government schools. The selection and placement of teachers working in the government schools is done by him. In the recent years, in almost all districts, there has been no recruitment of teachers in government schools. Whenever vacancies arose, the District Educational Officers would recall the teachers sent on deputation to the Panchayati Raj bodies and absorb them.

In the case of Zilla Parishad and Panchayat Samithi schools, the selection of teachers is done by the district selection committee. It consisted of Zilla Parishad Chairman, District Development Officer and three non-officials (nominated by government) as members. The District Collector acts as

Chairman of the Committee. The placement of teachers is done by the respective managements (i.e., Zilla Parishad and Panchayat Samithis) in accordance with their requirements. The selection and transfers of teachers in Panchayati Raj bodies generally depend on the whims and fancies of the non-officials.

In the case of Private Aided Schools, the District Educational Officer is made a member of the selection committee though he does not have any voting power. All the schools are supposed to obtain a list of applicants from the District Employment Exchange but this rule is often not adhered to. The working conditions and the service regulations are not always very attractive. The Employment Exchanges, therefore, do not evince any interest in the employment potential of these schools. In addition, the teachers are posted on purely adhoc basis for short spell of time. The unemployed youth, therefore, do not evince much interest in taking assignment in private schools. For sanctioning of new posts in all types of schools, the District Educational Officer has to forward the proposals to the directorate.

B. Salary Administration

Salaries of school teachers are disbursed in three different ways under the three different kinds of managments, viz., government, local bodies and private management. There is the provision of post-auditing for government schools and pre-auditing for schools under local bodies. The pre-auditing is done by the District Treasury of the Local Fund Authority. And there is also regular audit by Local Fund Examiner and the Accountant Generals' Auditors.

In the urban schools the Deputy Inspectors of the Schools of the area has to function as the drawing officers for all Primary Schools. For Upper Primary Schools, the Headmasters concerned draw the amount and disburse it among the teachers of the schools. In the case of Panchayat Samithi Schools, the headmasters of the Central Schools (or the Pay Units) draw the salary and disbursement is made among the teachers of schools which are under its purview.

The gazetted and non-gazetted headmasters of Secondary Schools have to draw the salaries of their staff on their own. Regarding aided schools, every year the Director of School Education has to release the amount, on the letter of credit issued against the sanctioned provision.

C. Promotions

In the case of government schools, the District Educational Officer has a crucial role in promotion of teachers. He is made the promoting authority up to the level of school assistants grade-II. The promotion of grade-I school assistants is effected by Regional Joint Director of School Education. Every year the headmasters of the schools have to send confidential reports of their teachers to the District Educational Officer, who would maintain the seniority lists of teachers. The Parishad Educational Officer and the District Development Officer are made important authorities so far as the promotion of the teachers of Zilla Parishad School is concerned. The criteria for promotion were seniority and merit.

D. Transfers

Transfer of the teachar is another crucial factor in management of schools. It is considered as a mechanism to control the teachers. Transfers of the teachers are made by the managements concerned. There is a rule that no teacher should be transferred in the middle of an academic year. But there have been instances in Andhra Pradesh, where teachers were transferred as many as six times a year. And there are instances where teachers who have stayed more than six years in their native place.[11] Transfers of teachers from one Zilla Parishad area to another Zilla Parishad area is made in consultation with the Directorate of School Education. Inter Samithi transfers of teachers are done through Zilla Parishad. In both the cases it is done only if there arises a vacancy. Transfers of teachers of Zilla Parishad Secondary Schools are effected by District Development Officer. The transfer of teachers of Panchayat Samithi School is made by Block Development Officer. The transfers of government school teacners are made by the District Educational Officer.

E. Pension and Provident Fund

In the case of pension, the proposals of Panchayati Raj School Teachers appointed by the District Educational Officer in pre-Panchayati Raj period, should first go to Block Development Officer for verification. The Block Development Officer would forward the papers to the District Educational Officer who would scrutinise and forward them to the Accountant General. The Accountant General has to accord sanction for the pension amount and write to the District Treasury Officer, who would release the amount to the pensioner every month. The proposals of teachers appointed after the formation of Panchayati Raj, are sent to the Panchayat Samithi. The Samithi will in turn send them to Zilla parishad. At Zilla Parishad the proposals are finalised and pension amount is given to the candidate. But till the time of this study there was no case of a retired teacher under Panchayati Raj bodies in the district.

In the case of Provident Fund, the proposals of the government teachers working in Panchayati Raj bodies are sent to Block Development Officer, who in turn would send them to Accountant Generals Office (where the accounts of the teachers are maintained), through District Educational Officer. The Accountant Generals' Office would send cheques to teachers, whereas the accounts of Panchayati Raj teachers are maintained at the Zilla Parishad.

F. Grievance Machinery

The teachers associations play a significant role in solving the grievances of their members. Mostly they handle the collective issues of teachers. There are a number of associations working in different parts of the state. They negotiate at all levels—the District, the Directorate, and the Secretariat and even at the Ministers level. The District Education Officer is made the first appellate authority for individual cases. Since the District Educational Officer is not in a position to take any action against the managements, the Directorate and some times the Secretariat have to interfere in the cases.[12]

In the case of Samithi teachers, some small issues like transfers, promotions are dealt by the Block Development Officer on receiving an application from the teachers.

2. Finance

There exists a provision for education cess. But at present, the education cess is not passed on to Panchayati Raj bodies towards the maintenance of the educational institutions. The cost of establishment of primary and secondary education including contingencies is being met directly by the government. For this purpose the Education Department would make the necessary provision in the state budget and funds are adjusted to the accounts of respective institutions after pre-audit by the Accounts Officer of the Local Fund Department.[13]

The District Education Officer releases grants to different managements and is expected to see that the funds are used properly. There is an auditor in the District Education Office to settle the accounts at the end of the financial year. Different managements would send their annual budget proposals with the necessary data to the District Education Officer. He has to pool them and send them to the Directorate for the preparation of the final budget.

The Salary bills of the aided and local body schools are borne entirely by the Education Department. Granting of aid to a school is decided by the Secretariat. On the suggestion and recommendation of the District Education Office, grant-in-aid is provided to the schools under private management. The District Educational Office has to advance the funds to the aided schools.

Certain norms are prescribed for giving grants-in-aid to schools. The school should be a recognised one. Trained staff, laboratory facilities, library, sanitary facilities, minimum enrolment of the students in the school, medium of instruction, physical facilities available in the school, location of the school and character of the management are some of the norms on the basis of which grant-in-aid is provided. The schools should also agree to abide by the government rules and accept the regular audit by the government. The District

Education Officer is made the final authority to recommend the cases to the Director of School Education. The recognition of the schools except English Medium, upto Primary are done by the District Educational Officer. Recognition of the English Medium Primary Schools and Secondary Schools has been accorded by the Director of School Education. But after formation of the Regional Joint Director of School Education, this job of granting recognition to English Medium schools is entrusted to him.

Grant-in-aid involves substantial expenditure on a recurring basis. Therefore, proposals are referred to the state government so that appropriate provision is made in the State budget.

In the case of Panchayati Raj Schools the Block Development Officer at the end of each financial year has to send proposals to District Educational Officer for grants. He in turn would release the amounts to schools in the shape of cash or kind.

The District Education Officer would process requirements for sanctioning of new posts and for additional grants for specific purposes. He would only process requests for admitting a school for the purpose of grant-in-aid but does not have any decision-making powers in this regard.

3. Academic

In educational administration, the most important activity at the field level is inspection of schools. The Deputy Educational Officer, the Deputy Inspectors and Junior Deputy Inspectors of Schools and Extension Officer (Education.,) spend most of the time in conducting inspections. They have heavy inspection schedules for evaluating the standards and methodology of teaching, physical conditions, etc. Their inspection can be categorised into three types :

1. Annual Inspection or Detailed Inspection
2. Follow-up-visits and
3. Surprise visits

The Inspectors have to examine numerous records, evaluate various facilities and physical conditions, assess the efficiency of teachers in the class, and also examine the methods used in teaching. While sending their inspection reports to the District Educational Officer and to management concerned, they have to send a copy of the report to the headmasters of the schools concerned. The management is expected to take follow-up-action on the inspection reports. The schools also have to send a 'Rectification Report' to the District Educational Officer about the action thev have taken on the inspection report. But in reality these reports do not lead to any follow-up-action.

The dual control of academic inspection of Panchayati Raj Schools by Deputy Education Officers and Deputy Inspectors of Schools on one hand, and administrative control by Parishad Educational Officer and Extension Officer (Education.,) on the other is causing lack of co-ordination among the inspecting officials. Teachers also do not bother about the inspection. The reason is that they are only the inspecting authority but the action on their reports depends upon will and pleasure of Panchayati Raj officials, who generally do not go through the inspection reports. The District Educational Officer has to supervise the inspection activites in the district, but it is just impossible for him to go through all the reports. As there are quite a large number of villages—eleven hundred in number—it is not possible to go through all the reports carefully. In addition, District Educational Officer has a number of additional responsibilities like inspection of High Schools, Junior Colleges and conducting examinations at regular intervals. Under these circumstances it is but natural for the inspection reports to gather dust in the office racks.

Yet another important academic activity at the district level is conducting examination for class VII. The District Educational Officer with the help of his inspecting staff, has to look after all the activities involved in it. They include appointment of paper setters, supervision over examination centres, appointment of examiners, tabulation of marks and announcement of results.

In addition to this District Educational Officer has to help the Secretary S.S.C. Board in conducting examinations for Class-X. He has to send the seniority list of teachers for the appointment of examiners, supervise the examination centres, distribute question papers and also help in spot valuation and tabulation of marks.

For academic activities the District Educational Officer acts as a link between schools and the state level machinery. He has the responsibility of supervising the distribution of nationalised text-books, recommending the schools for recognition by the Directorate, and helping in the implementation of new schemes.

The above discussion shows that, there were no problems in salary administration, promotion, pension and provident fund because these activities are based on mechanical and routine practices. But the selection, placement and transfers of the teachers appear to be problematic with the involvement of politics and favouritism. In these cases teachers become victims of whims and fancies of officials and non-officials. Ragarding grievances of teachers, there is no separate grievance machinery to deal with their difficulties. Though there are teachers unions to negotiate, they do not evince much interest in individual problems of teachers. Regarding finances also. though Panchayati Raj bodies are entrusted with the administrative powers, they have no independent source of income to spend on education. They have to depend entirely on government and spend in accordance with the government instructions.

4. Other Activities of Field Level Administration

The other activities of field level administration mainly includes welfare activities such as administration of mid-day meal programme, supply of text-books to the schools and distribution scholarships and other free aids. Here each of these aspects are discussed in detailed.

A. Administration of Mid-day Meal Programme

Since the details of the programme are discussed in a separate chapter, only the administrative machinery is presented here. Mid-day meal programme implemented in the district from its inception in November, 1982 to its abolition in 1985. At the district level, District Collector was the overall incharge for implementing the scheme. The civil supplies department and the revenue department of the district were incharge of distributing the rice, pulses and edible oils to the schools. At the field level, during 1982-83 the concerned school headmasters were made incharge for getting the food cooked and its distribution to the students. In view of the complaint that the teachers were overburdened with mid-day meals programme, during the year 1983-84, the programme was handed over to Sarpanchas, Voluntary Organizations and Municipalities. The Municipalities in the district expressed their inability to implement the programme. In some of the villages neither the Surpanchas nor the voluntary agencies came forward to implement the programme. Consequently there is no mid-day meal programme in those villages.[14] The edible oil was supplied to mid-day meal centres through Fair Price Shops, and the rice and pulses are handed over to Samithi. Samithi in turn would distribute them to the village centres through E.O. (Edn.,). Previously when teachers were implementing the programme the Samithi and Education Department of the district were having full control over the implementation of the programme. As the Surpanchas happen to be non-officials, there was no control over them. The implementation of the programme largely depended on their willingness. The Extension Officer (Edn.,) and Deputy Inspector of Schools felt that they can only visit the mid-day meal centres and note it in the inspection reports, but they do not have any authority to take action against irregularities in implementing the programme. Most of the Surpanchas have not implemented the programme themselves. They made somebody incharge of it who did not evince any interest in feeding the pupils. In most of the villages there were irregularities in the implementation of the programme.

B. Text-book Supply to the Schools

In view of the irregularities committed by book sellers, and non-availability of books in time, the government took upon the responsibility to distribute the books and note books to all the schools. Text books were supplied by the regional sales book depot of Andhra Pradesh Text Books, situated at the district headquarters, to the Deputy Inspectors of Schools on credit basis. Each school has to send its requirements to the Deputy Inspector of Schools concerned. Taking the requirements of all the schools under his jurisdiction, the Deputy Inspector indicates his requirements to the regional sales depot. The Deputy Inspectors have to collect the required books from the depot and distribute them to the schools on credit basis. The headmasters of the school have to collect the required books from Deputy Inspector concerned and sell them to the students and hand over the money to the Deputy Inspector who in turn hand it over to the sales depot. Earlier the High School headmasters were directly approaching the sales depot but later they changed that system. With the result headmasters are made to collect books from Deputy Inspector of Schools of the area. The process of supply of note-books is also the same, but distributor of note-books is A.P. State Trading Corporation. At the school level headmasters are made incharge of getting and selling of books and note-books to the students. Deputy Inspectors and headmasters are paid 4% on the amount they got from selling books toward conveyance charges.

The headmasters and Deputy Inspectors were facing some problems in the process of distribution. Sufficient number of books are not always available in sales depot, they had to go round to the depot several times to collect the books. The books would not come in time. That creates problems in the school. These transactions related to books is additional burden on these functionaries adversely affecting their regular activities.

C. Distribution of Scholarships, Dresses, Free Books etc.

In order to ensure more and more enrolment and retention of children in schools and to give a helping hand to poor, a provision is created for distribution of scholarships, free degree, free school bags, free books by the District Social Welfare and Tribal Welfare departments. All headmasters of schools forward applications of students of the Scheduled Caste, backward caste, economically backward classes and the Scheduled Tribes to social welfare and tribal welfare officers of the district. They have to sanction the amount or goods for the beneficiary pupils through the headmasters.

There were several problems in this scheme. The free books often come in less number. They come very late, forcing the pupils to purchase the books in the market. Sometimes books would come after most of the syllabus is over. Scholarships also come very late. The amount of scholarship is meagre and sometimes it is paid in instalments. The dresses and bags are poor in quality and there are instances where they did not last for more than three months

An analysis of administration of these welfare activities also shows that the mid-day meal programme suffered a great deal on account of inadequate machinery to implement it. The teachers and village Surpanchas, who are entrusted with this job, lacked interest in it. They felt that it is an additional burden on them. The scheme also sufferred from lack of equipment to prepare meals and to serve it. The supply of text-books also became a burden on school and teachers were unhappy with it. The parents were unhappy with the poor quality of dresses and meagre amount of scholarships. Hence these activities also did not cope with the objective of universal education.

5. Physical Equipment

Most of the schools in the district are not having adequate accommodation. Most of the classes are run under the shade of trees or in varandas. The worst effected are the Primary schools and single-teacher schools. Though the high school have laboratories, they were not accurately and properly equipped. There are no good library facilities in the schools. Though the high schools have their own libraries, most of them have become disfunctional because of lack of sufficient books, lack of library rooms etc. Regarding the games facilities, only high schools were some what equipped with games materials such as volleyball, ball badminton, etc. A good number of high schools did not have teachers of Physical Education Training. Some other teacher is made incharge of games who neither finds time nor shows any interest in games. Regarding the furniture only high schools were having some furniture although it was neither adequate nor in good condition. In the Primary Schools and single-teacher schools virtually there has been no furniture except one or two chairs, one or two wooden boxes, and one or two broken black boards. An overwhelming majority of pupils are made to sit on the floor with full of dust. Though in the budget of the rural schools 6% to the total salary bill is meant for furniture, that amount is neither sufficient nor released totally. In the government schools even that provision does not exist.

The financial position of the schools is found very bad. Their financial resources are quite meagre. The only source was the contingent amount and the tuition fee paid by few forward class pupils. This is not enough to maintain the school for the whole year. For they need to spend on purchasing chalk pieces, dusters, white papers for official use, water pots, etc. The number of teachers in the district was also inadequate. Most of the schools did not have mathematics teachers, craft instructors, games teachers, etc. The worst hit were Primary Schools and single-teacher schools where one teacher has to handle more than two classes at a time and engage the students the whole day.

Though a few students of the Scheduled Castes, Scheduled Tribes and Backward Castes benefit from the social welfare and tribal welfare departments, the amounts they get in the name of scholarships was inadequate. The clothes, school bags etc., were of poor quality. The free books they get were inadequate in number and did not get them in time. There was no sanitation and drinking water facility in the rural schools. With the result, girls students are put to terrible inconvenience.

In order to have an insight into the problem of physical equipment of schools, an attempt is made to examine the physical conditions of the schools at a micro level. For this purpose one single-teacher primary school of 'Peta' village, Upper Primary School of 'Konda' village and one Upper Primary School and one Secondary School of 'Kur' village are covered.

A. Accommodation

Accommodation is the basic requirement of any school. In addition to several other advantages, good accommodation has been one of the attractions for the success of private schools even in the rural areas. Because of inadequate accommodation, the rural schools do not inspire the confidence of the people. A good building can generate a school atmosphere in the village.

At the time of the study, there was no accommodation at all in the 'Peta' village where there was a single-teacher school.[15] There was only a few yards of space provided for the school in the centre of the village. A hut of a very small size was constructed every year with the help of people. It collapses almost every year and requires to be raised periodically. There were no walls and doors to the school and sometimes it had no roof. The little hut hardly accommodates 15 to 20 children. The teacher cannot stand on his feet in the school as the roof hits his head because of its low hight. The children were always exposed to sun, wind, and rain. The rainy days and sunny days were holidays to school children. The stormy wind kicks off dust in the faces of little kids. Though some trials were made for construction of a school building, it did not materialise partly because no contractor came forward to undertake construction and partly the village elite had no interest in the construction of school building. The contractor was not interested because he does not earn much profit and the elite were not interested because their children were not studying in these schools.

The 'Konda' village, where there was a primary school, the situation was no different. There were three schools on paper, all of them operating under one shelter. It had six classes with a total strength of 300 students. There were only three rooms ; one of which was a Gram Panchayat room. Of these three rooms one was converted into store room with the introduction of mid-day meal scheme. Apart from them there were also two varandas attached to the school. Classes were also run in these varandas. Four classes were accommodated in rooms and varandas and two classes (class I & II) always run under trees (one was run under the shade of a tree and another under the shade of walls of a nearby house). Recently class VII was added without providing for additional accommodation. Even a drizzle upsets the teaching schedule and the children are let off. There was also a staff from which was also used a class room.[16]

The story of accommodation of school in 'Kur' village was no different. Though there were two separate schools i.e., one secondary school and one Upper Primay School, only the Secondary School has some accommodation, ofcourse insufficient. The school also had no library room. The books, though very few, were kept in an almirah which is kept in a class room. The staff room was very congested to accommodate all the teachers. The Upper Primary School of the village was the worst in respect of accommodation. A very small room was being used by the Headmaster and the staff. There were in all 14 teachers. The room cannot accommodate more than five teachers at a time. There were class rooms only for VI and VII classes. The V class was accommodated in on old room. The IV class was run in the varanda. The other classes constituting nearly half of the school student population sit under the shade of tree or shadow of the walls of the school. The floor is quite dusty. The dust is thrown into the faces of the children as pointed out earlier. The students who sit under the trees have to constantly move around the tree as the direction of the shade changes. All the rainy days were actually holidays to the primary sections of the school. The school is situated near the village bus stop. All the vehicles that ply on the road, not only detract the attention of the students, but also throw a lot of dust on their faces. As four classes were conducted simultaneously in the open ground, one class disturbs the other whenever a teacher is absent or does not take the class.[17] It is in this situation the little children have to pursue their education in the rural areas.

B. Furniture, Laboratory, Library and Games

There was no sufficient furniture in any of the school under study. In 'Peta' village, there was no furniture except one old wooden chair for the teacher to sit and a small black-board. All the pupils have to sit on dusty floor except a few who get their own small mats to sit.

There was not even a wooden box to maintain the school records. The teacher ties the school records with a rope and keeps them in a neighbouring house. There were no teaching aids at all in the school like charts and maps. There was no games material and library book is an unknown word to them.

The 'Konda' village Upper Primary School, with seven classes and more than 300 students and six teachers, had only one table, four chairs and two stools. Two teachers sit on stools in the class rooms as there were no chairs. There were two wooden boxes in the school to keep the school records. They were also used for sitting purpose whenever some visitors come to the school. The students used to sit on the floor as there were no benches There were about ten desks to be used by the students while writing something in their note-books. There were two small wooden almirahs in the school to keep the science equipment and teaching aids. There were only four black-boards for all the seven classes in the school. A few classes go without black boards. There were a few teaching aids in the school like Telugu, Hindi and English alphabet charts and a few exhibits with moral stores and science charts. Though there was nothing like a laboratory in the school there were a few science apparatus like bell jar, beaker, test tubes etc., without any chemicals. There were no library books in the school nor any games material.

In 'Kur' village the secondary school had some furniture. There were 13 chairs and 72 benches to facilitate the seating arrangement for 12 teachers and 280 students. There were 9 tables and 5 stools in the school. There were only two black-boards with stands, the remaining boards were attached to the class room walls. There were 8 almirahs to keep records of admission, examination, etc., and also to keep science material and library books There were four wooden boxes, one wall clock and one typewriter in the school. In addition to these equipment there was a mike set, one ceiling fan in Head-

Master's office and one duplicator. There were two globes and some geographical and science maps in the school. There was a laboratory room in the school. Though there was some science equipment, it was not useful to undertake any experiment. Most of it was in broken pieces without any use. They were useful only to show to the students, but not to make use of them for experiments. Such material included a beaker, burratt, china dish, washing bottle, fired jar glass, bell jar, kipps apparatus, human skeleton, biological maps, meter scale, magnate, rubber tube, clinical thermo-metre, dry cell, telescope, saw, hammar, cutting pair, hand drilling machine, heat chest, mirror, periscope, sundial watch, catelen lamp, simple spring balance, common balance, simple pully, hydro metre, projector, siphon formula and telescope. All these science material exists but not useful for practical purposes. All of them are very old, broken and useless. Though there was chemistry equipment in the school, there were no chemicals and acids in the school. Regarding games, there was a physical education teacher in the Secondary School, and games material which includes two voueyball ball badminton nets and bats, four rings, two chess boards, six skippings, one shot-put ball and two high jump poles in the school.

The furniture and accommodation of Upper Primary School of 'Kur' village was equally in bad shape. There were about fourteen chairs and two tables in the school. Only the pupils of VII class were having the luxury of sitting on the benches. The remaining pupils had to sit on floor which becomes very dirty during the rainy season. There were five black-boards with stand and four wall boards. There were two almirahs and two wooden boxes to keep the school records and attendance registers. There were a very few maps and charts in the school. There was no laboratory or science material. There was no library or library books. There was neither a games teachers nor games material.[18] This speaks of the ill-equipped character of some of these rural schools.

C. Sanitation and Drinking Water

There was no sanitation and drinking water facility in any of the schools under study. In 'Peta' village where there was no school building, the questions of drinking water and sanitation does not arise. There was not even a pot to store the water for drinking purposes. If the children felt thirsty, they had to rush to their houses for water.

There was no sanitation and drinking water facility in the schools of 'Konda' and 'Kur' villages also. These two villages suffer from water scarcity during all the seasons, more so during the summer. People quarelling at drinking water wells is a common scene. Since there was water scarcity boys had to go only to their houses for water. Since they are big villages all the children cannot go to their houses every time, because of the distance. The students have to go to nearby house to ask for drinking water. Very often the people of neighbouring houses refuse to give water to students because of water scarcity. If the children go upto to the well for water, the men and women are so busy in drawing their own water from the wells that they do not care to offer water to these school children. On the other hand they get annoyed if they ask for water. Absence of sanitation facilities put the girl students to enormous inconvenience. They have to walk more than one to two furlongs in search of privacy to attend to nature's calls.

D. Teaching Staff

There was inadequate number of teaching staff in all the villages, In 'Peta' village since it was a single teacher school, one teacher had to handle all the subjects of all classes. The inability of the teacher to deal with all the subjects leads to negligence of the education. As it has been rightly pointed out in the Sixty First report of the Estimates Committee (1983-84) on elementary education in India, that "many single-teacher schools are in fact no teacher schools".[19] The problem with the single teacher schools has been whenever the only teacher fails to attend the school, the school would remain closed.

In 'Konda' village there were six teachers for seven classes. The staff was completely inadequate to the teaching requirements of the school. Every time one or two classes go without teacher. If any teacher goes on leave, the problem becomes much worse, resulting in more classes going without teacher. Further there was no games teacher nor a craft teacher in the school.

In 'Kur' village, though the Secondary School had sufficient staff, the Upper Primary School was suffering from inadequate number of staff. Though there were fourteen teachers in the school, they were not sufficient in view of several sections with a strength of 700. Even in this school there was no games and crafts teacher.

Added to the problem of inadequate number of teachers, almost all the teachers commute to the village every day. Hence most of them were irregular in attending schools or come very late. This would obviously effect the entire education.

E. Welfare Activities

Government has been undertaking certain welfare activities for school children. This includes scholarships, free books, dresses, school bags and slates, etc., to backward class, Scheduled Tribe, Scheduled aste and Ceconomically backward class students. Since long back, the pupils of 'Peta' village school have not been granted any of the above benefits, because of lack of interest on the part of the teachers.

In 'Konda' village, the Scheduled Caste pupil of class I and class II were getting Rs. 15 per year as scholarship and one dress, one school bag, and slate and slate pencils—all put together not more than Rs. 30 worth. They were also entitled for free books. All the Scheduled Caste students of classes III to V get every year Rs. 45 each as scholarship and a few free books. No scholarships were sanctioned to any of the backward class or other poor students.

In Upper Primary School of 'Kur' village also each Scheduled Caste boy of class I and class II use to get every year Rs. 15, one dress, slate and slate pencils, school bag and free books. The Scheduled Caste students of above class III to V get Rs. 45 and class VI and VII get Rs. 50 each and free books. A few students of backward class also get Rs. 45 to Rs. 50 per year as scholarship. The students of secondary school of the village get several types of scholarships. This include merit scholarship, aid for physically handicapped students, and riyayathi scholarships.

Though a few students did get some monetary relief due to welfare measures undertaken by the government, the relief is considered to be inadequate. Scheduled Caste students of class I and II get a sum of Rs. 15 per year as scholarships that too, some times they are paid in two instalments Rs. 8 at one time and Rs. 7 at another time. The study reveals that the dresses and school bags they get are of very poor quality. Most of the time they do not fit to the physique of the students. They are either loose or tight. The free books often come very late. Out of four to six subjects only one or two books are given. They have to buy the remaining books in the market.

Summing-Up

The above analysis of administrative set up for education shows that the present set up is evolved from the colonial British rule and the princely state of Hyderabad and the composite state of Madras. Though from time to time some changes were effected in the administrative set up, they have been of a very peripheral nature. Till 1965 there were administrative units at state, regional and field levels. It was in 1965 the regional level was abolished and the district level was sought to be strengthened by elevating the position of District Educational Officer to the status of Deputy Director. However, a regional set up with Regional Joint Directors was established again in 1982.

Constant changes have been taking place from time to time in the state level set up like bifurcation, unification and rebifurcation of Directorate of Public Instruction. But no significant changes have been effected at grassroots level since 1965 onwards.

The introduction of Panchayati Raj system and placing a large number of schools under it is considered a significant development in the evolution of educational administration. This system came under severe criticism for various corners as it failed to accomplish the objectives of universalisation of education on the one hand and democratic decentralization of administration on the other.

The discussion with officials of Panchayati Raj Schools reveals that the government has a tight grip over Panchayati Raj Schools in view of its financial commitment. In academic matters, in the name of technical control the government exercises detailed control. This prevents the Panchayati Raj Schools from their independent development.

Administratively they are under Panchayati Raj Institutions and technically under Education Department. The salaries of the teachers are paid by the government, while the Panchayati Raj bodies exercise day-to-day administrative control. Due to dual management, neither the government has full control nor the Panchayati Raj. The Panchayati Raj teachers do not take the inspecting authority seriously as the disciplinary action is to be initiated by Panchayati Raj bodies. Thus the administration suffers in terms of administrative control.

While the administrative set up is having several deficiencies, the physical equipment of the schools is not adequate for promotion of healthy education in rural areas. An analysis of the physical conditions of the schools reveals that they suffer from lack of accommodation, furniture, sanitation facilities, library books, science equipment and inadequate and poor quality of government assistance. The smaller the school, the more it suffers.

The defective administrative machinery, weak grassroots management, and poor physical conditions reduce the quality and quantity of education in rural areas. Such school management cannot attain either universalization of education, nor can create skilled man power in the rural sector.

REFERENCES

1. The other Regional Joint Directors of Higher Education were located at Cuddapah, Rajahmundry and Guntur.
2. The other Regional Joint Directors of School Education were located at Guntur, Cuddapah, Kakinada and Hyderabad.
3. Recently the Zilla Parishads were renamed as Zilla Praja Parishads.
4. More or less the same type of set-up was retained in the Mandal system which was introduced latter.

5. N.B.—5 per cent of the number of institutions in each category should be visited in a year.
6. As per 1976 Amendment to the Act, Education Committee is the second standing Committee among five Committees of Zilla Parishad.
7. With the abolition of Panchayat Samithis, the Mandal Panchayats were made responsible for these schools.
8. See *Working Paper on Panchayati Raj Institutions*; State Committee on Panchayati Raj, Government of A.P., 1980, p. 47.
9. More or less the same type of position and functions were retained the new Mandal set-up also.
10.]in For details see, *Andhra Pradesh Gram Panchayats Act*, 1964 (Act No. 2 of 1964) As amended upto 31st December, 1978, Government Central Press, Government of Andhra Pradesh, Hyderabad, 1978, p. 43.
11. Dharni, P. Sinha, *Descriptive-cum-Critical Study of Education in Andhra Pradesh*, Administrative Staff College of India, Hyderabad, 1976, p. 152.
12. *Ibid.*, pp. 153-154.
13. *Working Paper on Panchayati Raj Institutions, op. cit.*, p. 93.
14. Out of 1647 centres in the District, only 1224 were functioning.
15. Very recently one room building was constructed and one more teacher was posted in this school. The other things remained the same.
16. Very recently two more classes and two more rooms were added, but the other conditions remained the same.
17. Even now the situation continues to be more or less the same.
18. Even now the situation regarding furniture and other equipmen continue to be more or less the same in all the schools studied.
19. See editorial on 'Schooling lags', *Indian Express*, Daily March 5, 1984, p. 8.

4

Problems and Perceptions of Teachers

Teachers constitute an important segment of school education and its administration. The success or failure of the school education depends upon the interest evinced by teachers. The behaviour of students also depends on the overall performance of their teacher. For a rural child, teacher is supposed to be a reference model. The Indian Education Commission 1964-66 felt that "Of all the different factors which influence the quality of education and its contribution to national development, the quality, competence and character of teachers is undoubtedly the most significant. Nothing is more important than securing a sufficient supply of high quality recruits to the teaching profession, providing them with the best possible professional preparation and creating satisfactory conditions of work in which they can be fully effective".[1] Teachers being such an important factor, and the process of education being class room based, their problems need a detailed examination.

Another dimension that deserves a detailed examination is the participation of the teacher in educational management. It has been observed that they are never involved in preparation of plans, curriculum and text-books and their opinions and problems have never been taken into consideration while making the decisions with respect to education. In this regard, J.P. Naik maintained that "this non-involvement of teachers in preparation and implementation of educational plans is one of the major weaknesses in our system and unless it is effectively remedied, it will not be possible to promote the development of education in a big way".[2] In this regard an attempt is made to examine the problems of teachers and their perceptions on various aspects of rural education and their participation in the educational process. The chapter seeks to examine the conduciveness of the system to achieve the policy objective of achieving universal education.

This chapter covers the teachers of the three village schools under study. There were in all thirty three teachers in these three schools. The views of thirty two teachers elicited through a questionnaire and informal discussions are presented here. However, one teacher declined to respond. The following is the analysis emerging from these interviews. Of the thirty two teachers, one teacher belongs to Primary School (i.e., single-teacher school) of 'Peta' village, six belong to Upper Pramriy School and eleven to Zilla Parishad Secondary School of 'Kur' village. Of the thirty two teachers five teachers are female teachers.

I. Social Background of the Teachers

Social background of the teachers is important. It provides the profile through which one can examine the relation between the teachers and their social environment. For this purpose the particulars of caste, occupation, qualifications, and rural/urban background are collected.

TABLE 4.1

Caste Background of Teachers

Caste	Frequency	Percentage
Forward Cast	6	18.75
Backward Caste	23	71.87
Scheduled Caste	3	9.38
Total	32	100.00

The caste background of the thirty two teachers under study shows that, an overwhelming majority of them (72 per cent) belong to backward castes like Padmasali, Gouda, Perika, Batraju, Jangam, Vadla, etc. About 19 per cent belong to forward castes like Reddy, Brahmin, Vyshya and remaining 9 per cent of the teachers come from the Scheduled Castes. No teacher comes from the Scheduled Tribe community.

TABLE 4.2

Secondary Occupation of Teachers

Occupation	Frequency	Percentage
No other occupation	23	71.88
Agriculture	7	21.87
Others	2	6.25
Total	32	100.00

The above table indicates that an overwhelming majority (71.87 per cent) of teachers had no other occupation. From the remaining teachers about 22 per cent had agriculture, and about six per cent had the other occupations like petty trading and medical practice.

TABLE 4.3

Education and Training of Teachers

Education and Training	Frequency	Percentage
Trained Middle	4	12.50
Trained Matriculates or HSC	7	21.88
Trained Inter or P.U.C.	5	15.62
Trained Graduates	11	34.38
Untrained Graduates	2	6.25
Trained Post-Graduates	3	9.37
Total	32	100.00

The education and training levels of teachers shows that most of the teachers were graduates with B. Ed. or SGBT Training. There 21were per cent of the teachers with H.S.C. and SGBT Training. There were also two non-trained graduate teachers and two P.G. teachers. Some teachers were educated upto middle with SGBT or EGBT Training, and some were educated upto P.U.C. or Intermediate with SGBT or EGBT Training. On the whole except two teachers, all have undergone one or the other type of training.

The birth place and place of education of teachers (Table 4.4) shows that 28 per cent are born in urban areas, i.e., the headquarters of a district, and the remaining teachers are born in rural areas. Although only 28 per cent are born in the urban areas, about 45 per cent of the teachers are entirely educated in urban areas. From among the rest, most of them are partly educated in urban areas and partly in rural areas. A few teachers completed their entire education in rural areas. The teachers of this generation had to go to cities to pursue even middle level education as the schools in rural areas were rare in those days.

TABLE 4.4

Rural-Urban Background of Teachers

Rural/Urban	Frequency	Percentage
Born in Rural Areas	23	71.87
Born in Urban Areas	9	28.13
	32	100.00
Educated in Rural Areas	5	15.63
Educated in Urban Areas	14	43.75
Educated Partly Rural and partly Urban	13	40.62
Total	32	100.00

About the parental education of the teachers, the table 4.5 indicates that about 37 per cent of the fathers and 84 per cent of the mothers of the teachers belong to illiterate category. About 41 per cent of the fathers and 13 per cent of the mothers are educated upto Primary level and only 21 per cent of the fathers and 3 per cent of the mothers completed high school education. No mother and father of any teacher is educated upto the college level. This shows that generally the teaching jobs attract only middle and lower middle class persons whose parents either are illiterate or a little educated.

TABLE 4.5

Parental Education of Teachers

Level of Education	Father's Frequency	Education Percentage	Mother's Frequency	Education Percentage
Illiterate	12	37.50	27	84.38
Primary	13	40.63	4	12.50
Secondary	7	21.87	1	3.12
Total	32	100.00	32	100.00

To a question relating to their economic status, 87.5 per cent rated themselves as middle income group and the remaining 12.5 per cent categorised themselves as lower middle class. They mostly come from S.C. and B.C. families. Nobody claimed the status of upper middle or rich.

An analysis of the social background of teachers reveals that most of them come from backward castes, with a reasonable educational background. A large number of them belong to rural middle class or lower middle class families. Slightly more than one fifths of the teachers were engaged in other occupations also.

II. Infrastructure and Administrative Problems

To a question about adequacy of accommodation, furniture and teaching aids, only 6 per cent belonging to secondary schools said that they have the facilities. About 66 per cent, mostly of Upper Primary and Primary Schools, felt that they have none of these facilities. The rest of the teachers stated that the facilities exist but are not adequate. The following comments made by the teachers indicate the intensity of the problem.

One Secondary School teacher said "though, to some extent, we have class rooms, benches, library books and science equipment, nothing is useful for the present day requirements of the school education." Another teacher of a Upper Primary School said, "classes being run under the shade of the trees—dust raised by each bus falls on our faces—classes are let off in rainy season." The third teacher commented, "we have fourteen sections in all but there are only four class rooms. The remaining students are compelled to sit under trees. There is no library and laboratory in the school. All these factors are leading to declining interest among the students in education." The fourth one observed, "there is no school at all here, only there are teachers and students, nothing else." The fifth said, "there is no furniture in the school. we sit on wooden boxes because there are no chairs." The single-teacher school master commented "except one small black board, we have nothing, we have neither accommodation nor furniture, nor any other thing." This was the pattern of comments which indicate the intensity and the state of affairs in rural education.

When enquired about the facilities for children of their schools only 37.5 per cent felt that all the students have books, slates, etc. A majority from the remaining felt that S.Ts. and S.Cs. are not having books. Others felt that some sections of B.Cs. and F.Cs. are also not having books. On the whole a majority of the teachers felt that students are not having sufficient books and slates on account of poverty and inability of the government to distribute the books in time.

Regarding the distribution of text-books through governmental machinery and schools, more than 90 per cent of the teachers felt that inspite of government distributing the books, they never reach the schools within the stipulated time. The reasons they point out are delay in printing, frequent changes in syllabus and text-books, ineffective system of supply and inefficiency of government o deliver the books in time.

They have also made certain suggestions to improve the supply of text-books. These suggestions include ; directly sending the books to the schools without intermediary officials, books should reach the schools before or during the summer vacation itself, government should see that the printing activity is over well in advance. Some suggested delinking of text-books supply from schools and handing over them to separate book banks or private book-sellers in advance.

Most of them felt that there is a necessity of changing syllabus according to the changing situations and exploding knowledge. About 90 per cent of them felt that, though there is a need for change in books now and then, it is causing a lot of inconvenience to the students and teachers. They felt that the changed books are not reaching the schools in time. By the time the books arrive, more than half of the academic year is over. Most of the poor students cannot afford to buy new books every time. In villages most of the students buy the books previously used from their senior students for half of the rate. The change in text-books force the students to buy new books which costs more.

About the supply of free text-books to the schools, only 40 per cent were satisfied with the present supply of the text-books to the Scheduled Caste and Scheduled Tribe children. From the rest, a majority felt that the supply of free text-books is not satisfactory. Most of them felt that free-books come very late to the school. They supply books after six months of opening of the schools. By that time most of the Scheduled Caste pupils buy books in the market. Some teachers felt that only a section of the Scheduled Caste students get free books and others have to buy them in the market. They never supply sufficient number of books. The students who get books do not get full set. Some of the books have to be purchased in the market. Teachers felt that there are malpractices in the distribution of free-books. In the process of distribution the officials do not release all the books at the starting point and make fortune from it. Sometimes the village elite come to the school and demand free books to their children. Out of compulsions teachers hand over some books to village elite by denying the books to the deserving students.

Regarding the free distribution of school dresses and school bags to the Scheduled Caste and Scheduled Tribe students by the social welfare department, almost all the teachers felt that they lack quality and come very late and in inadequate number.

About the scholarship to the students, more than half of the teachers were satisfied with the system of distribution of scholarships. The remaining teachers complained that the scholarships are not reaching in time and deserving students are not getting the scholarships. They suspect malpractice in the sanctioning and distribution of scholarships.

Regarding games and sports 43 per cent of the teachers, mostly of Secondary School, felt a bit satisfied about it. The teachers of Upper Primary and Primary School said that neither there is a games teacher nor the equipment for the games.

When asked about the behaviour of inspecting staff who visit the school, more than half of them reported favourably about these inspections. The others felt that the inspectors are authoritarian and inspection is more a fault finding exercise than fact finding.

III. Teacher-Community Relations

Teacher-community relations are essential in rural areas, as the efficiency of the school depends upon the relations they maintain with the community. Schools cannot function in isolation. Hence the teachers' perception of their relations with other sections of people is presented here.

(a) Teacher-student relations

To a question about the relationships between teacher and students, about two-thirds of the teachers opined that they are changing. The other one-third of the teachers did not perceive much change in the relations. Almost all the teachers who stated that there is a change reported that the change has been of negative kind. Students are rebelling against teachers, they are not caring to learn, they are indisciplined, there is no mutual understanding, the 'Bhakti' towards the teachers is getting eroded and students are growing violent. The cause for change, according to them, lies in the external environment. Students, they maintain, are changing according to the changing times and societal change. Some teachers felt that non-detention system has had an adverse impact on their learning process. A few other felt that the discipline is getting eroded because community does not hold the teacher in high esteem. The other cause pointed out include ; teachers are indulging in politics, and the classes have become over crowded.

The above attitudinal pattern indicates the dominance of 'Banking' system[3] of education and the belief of teachers in the old notion of 'discipline'.[4] A bit of change in the behaviour of students upsets the teachers.

(b) Teacher-Villagers relations

To a question about the contact between the teachers and the villagers a majority of them stated that, villagers occasionally meet them. They come to the teachers for the reasons such as to know about the progress of their children, to know about functioning of the school, to attend the national festivals organised by the schools and to observe the mid-day meal programme, etc.

It is also attempted to know how the village elite treat the school teachers. Only one-third of the teachers reported that they are respected by the elite. The remaining of them said that they are neither respected nor insulted but treated normally. One teacher said that the village elite are annoyed of the teachers. The cause for such a treatment, according to the teacher is that the village elite have no respect for the teachers. A few teachers observed that village elite are jealous of the teachers as they entertain the idea that teachers are getting their salaries without performing their duties.

An attempt is also made to know the involvement of the teachers in politics and their contacts with politicians. About 68 per cent of the teachers said that they have no relationship with politics or politicians. From among the others a considerable number (15%) said that their relations with politicians are cordial. The others said that they have soft-corner towards some party or the other.

There were parents' committees, school development committees or parent-teacher committee in all schools to look after the affairs of school like accommodation, teaching arrangements and other facilities. When asked about the necessity of this parents' committee, all the teachers agreed that there is a need for such committees at the village level to look after the development of the village school and welfare of school children. They also think that the need for such a committee arises to resolve the problems of the school such as accommodation, upgradation of school, maintenance of discipline among children, providing facilities in the school like drinking water, making the children study well and to improve the attendance in the school.

When asked about the functioning of parental committees, about 12 per cent did not reply. About 30 per cent said that it is not functioning well. They observed that it is not a constructive body, "it is not interested in children's development", "they do not bother about the difficulties of the school." From among the others 22 per cent said that it is functioning in a normal way and another 22 per cent said that there was nothing wrong with it. The remaining few felt that it is helping the Headmaster in solving some problems of the school.

IV Problems and Attitudes of Teachers

In order to understand the problems of school education it is important to know the problems of the teachers such as appointment, transfers, promotion, retirement, benefits, social position, housing problems, etc. Of the thirty two teachers, 31 per cent are appointed by the government, i.e., by District Educational Officer. Though all these schools are Panchayati Raj schools there were teachers who are appointed by government because they were appointees during pre-Panchayati Raj period. The remaining teachers (69 per cent) were appointed by Panchayati Raj i.e., District Selection Committee.

These teachers have put in service ranging from six years to 36 years. Of them 40 per cent have put in 16 to 20 years of service, 19 per cent 10 to 15 years service, 15 per cent above 30 years of service, 12 per cent 6 to 10 years of service and 6 per cent and 8 per cent were having the service ranging 21 to 25 and 26 to 30 years of service respectively.

In order to know the pattern of commitment towards their profession, the teachers were asked the causes for joining the teaching profession. About 18 per cent of the teachers said that they have interest in teaching profession and consider it as an honourable job. Another 28 per cent joined the job as they could not get any other job. They stated that they joined to eke out livelihood. About 9 per cent joined as an opportunity arose in this field. Another 9 per cent joined to transmit education and skills to others. About 6 per cent joined this profession to develop their own level of education. They think this is the job where one can improve himself while teaching others. The remaining 18 per cent joined the job to do service to the nation by educating the people. This shows that most of the teachers joined the profession out of some interest.

When asked about the problems faced by the teachers in appointments, most of them stated that they had no problem. However, the following improvements suggested in the recruitment system, indirectly suggest the problems and processes in recruitment. 56 per cent of the teachers belonging to Panchayati Raj cadre pleaded for appointment by the state government, rather than by Panchayati Raj institutions. A few others said there should not be any corrupt practices in the recruitment. Recruitments should be made on the basis of merit, efficiency and written test. This broadly indicates their disapproval of the present method and reveals that the method in vogue does suffer from certain limitations.

In respect of transfers—another crucial area—the data reveals that the number of transfers range from one time to more than ten times in their services. About 9 per cent of the teachers were transferred once or twice in their service, about 20 per cent three to four times, 19 per cent five to six times, 9 per cent seven to eight times. And the other 2[illegible] per cent got transferred more than ten times during their service. The discussions also indicate that there are cases where teachers got transferred thrice in a year and there are also cases where a few teachers were retained at the same place for more than 7 year.

When enquired into the reasons for their transfers, about 37 per cent stated that the transfers were due to long-standing at one place. About 22 per cent said their transfers were on their request and will. Another 10 per cent said on account of promotion. The remaining teachers felt that their transfers were politically motivated, transferred due to selfishness of officials, transferred as the village officers were against them. One teacher felt that teachers who use influence are given full freedom and choice about the place of work. Those who do not have influence have to work in nook and corner of the district. Another teacher said "in a period of one month, I was transferred thrice." A few teachers who were transferred on their own request admitted that "their requests were conceded only when they used influence or money." One teacher reported that his application for transfer was not considered till he spent Rs. 400 on the concerned persons.

When asked to advice a better transfer policy, about 34 per cent of the teachers felt that every teacher should be transferred once in five years. If transfers are very frequent, it becomes difficult to understand the village environment, problems of the school and children of the place. 19 per cent of the teachers said that transfers should be once in three years. Another 19 per cent said that transfers should take place only on the request of the teacher. The rest felt that, transfers should be made with a forethought. The experienced officers such as District Educational Officer should be given power of transfer. They opposed the non-officials exercising the power of transfer of teachers. It was suggested that before transferring a person, his place of choice should also be taken into consideration.

Regarding their promotions, half of them got promotions, and another half did not. Most of the teachers who got promotions belong to the Secondary School. Among those who got promotions, about 19 per cent as School Assistant Grade II & I, 17 per cent to School Assistant level. One teacher got first grade Headmaster and other teacher got promoted to the level of Primary School Headmaster. The remaining teachers (above 25 per cent) got promoted from EGBT to SGBT level i.e , elementary grade to secondary grade.

When enquired into their problems regarding promotion, a considerable number (40 per cent) did not answer. About 28 per cent felt that they got promotions because they are qualified. About 15 per cent felt that they got promotions very late. Another 9 per cent felt that they could not get promotions though they have fulfilled the required length of service. The remaining teachers complained that those who have put in less service got promotions as a result of discrimination and preferential treatment.

When asked to suggest a better promotion policy, about 38 per cent suggested that promotion should be based on the qualification of the candidates. The other suggestions include, promotion should be given immediately after the person is qualified, promotions should be based on the qualifications and service of the candidates, 15 per cent favoured seniority as the sole basis of promotion. There were also suggestions for removal of favouritism and delay in promotions.

Retirement policy is an important factor while dealing with the employees in the formal sector. Persons do take into account retirement benefits before joining any service. A better retirement policy can attract better persons for the job. When asked about the problems of retirement, most of them thought that retirement generally creates economic problems. Therefore, they pleaded that the pension amount and other retirement benefits should be sanctioned in time. A few teachers suggested that one should own a house by the time he retires.

When enquired about the desirable retirement policy 37 per cent of the teachers opined that 55 years of age is the ideal age to retire. One teacher felt it should be 58 years. Few teachers (6.25 per cent) said retirement age should be 50 years or voluntary retirement after 15 years of service. About 9 per cent felt that they should be allowed to work until they become old and unable to handle their duties. Six per cent told that retirement age should be 60 years, or 30 to 35 years of service.

Housing accommodation is another major problem encountered by the teachers in the villages. A majority of the teachers face no problems as most of them were daily commuters or natives of the villages. The remaining (31 per cent) stated that they face the severe problem of housing as there are no houses constructed for rental purposes. The houses are not equipped with bare minimum facilities such as toilets, bath—rooms and drinking water. One Harijan teacher remarked that caste poses a problem in getting a house. Another Harijan teacher said that, while he was working in one village, he used to stay in gram panchayat office or in the school building itself due to the caste consciousness of the villagers. Others felt that water scarcity is an acute problem in the villages. They suggested that every village should have teachers' quarters besides the school building as in the case of Railways where the quarters are provided at each railway station.

An attempt to know the self perception of the teachers indicates that 34 per cent of the teachers placed the teaching profession in the first place as most respected profession as against 41 per cent who placed medical profession in the first place. In their view society pays utmost respect for medical profession. The remaining 25 per cent placed other professions such as revenue officials, politicians, businessmen, agricultural officials, excise officials and bankmen as the respected professions.

The respectable profession in their second priority is taken by engineering profession. About 41 per cent placed other professions mentioned above as second respectable professions in the society. 17 per cent placed medical profession as second respectable profession, only 3 per cent placed teachers in that position.

This indicates that teachers do not perceive teaching profession as respectable in comparison with either medical or engineering professions.

The above analysis of the problems of teachers reveal that most of them belong to Panchayati Raj and have put in more than 15 years of service. Most of them have joined the profession because they liked it and deserve to help the people through this job. Yet they do not rate the teaching profession very high. With regard to administrative problems there is a large scale dissatisfaction. In matters of recruitment, transfers they have problems. Regarding promotion 50 per cent did not get promotions. They also expressed the difficulties in getting retirement benefits. Regarding problem of housing though most of the people commute every day, the others face housing problems in rural areas. This indicates the teachers were not satisfied with their service matters and with the general conditions in rural areas.

V. Relevance of Present Education System

It is important to examine the teachers' view point with regard to the relevance of present education and its impact on society. Teachers' views on this aspect are elicited as they constitute the crucial element in the implementation of any educational programme. Their approach would determine the pace and vigour of implementation.

To start with, it is attempted to analyse their perceptions of objectives of education. For this purpose they were asked to list out the objectives of the present education. About 31 per cent opined that the objectives of the present education mainly revolve around livelihood of the people. 19 per cent said that education not only helps in fulfilling the minimum needs of day to day life, but helps in all round development of human beings. About 12 per cent stated that shaping the human behaviour and making them good citizens is the main objective of education. About 9 per cent teachers felt that the objective of education is to impart the duties of the citizen in making the society a civilized one. Another 9 per cent said that education can impart discipline, honesty and self-help in the people. The rest of the teachers thought that the objectives of education include providing the literacy, political and scientific knowledge, increasing the awareness of people, enabling them to eke their livelihood. This analysis shows that most of the teachers have their own concept of education. It indicates the nature of ambiguity in the perception of the goals.

When asked to comment on the relevance of books and their contents for the future life of the children, about 40 per cent gave a complete negative answer. They further expressed that this syallabus is not at all useful to the students; they are irrelevant to the present day needs of society. Moreover, the students are over burdened with the bigger dose of syllabus. About 19 per cent felt that this syllabus is partially relevant. The remaining 31 per cent felt that the present syllabus is useful to the students. They argued that it provides literacy and awareness to the students. It also enables them in securing their livelihood. On the whole a majority of the teachers opined that the present syllabus and books are not relevant to the students and their lives.

To the question about the methods to be followed in syllabus formation and deciding contents of books in order to make the books more relevant, they suggested several improvements. About 44 per cent of them suggested technical and vocationa education at the school level. The rest of the suggestions pertain to the basic interest and aptitude of the student, inclusion of topics related to science, environment and new inventions and inculcation of discipline, sense of nationalism and duty mindedness.

Regarding the involvement of teachers in preparation of the syallabus, almost all the teachers opined that they should be involved in preparing the syllabus and writing the text books. They suggested certain ways and methods to involve teachers in writing text books. The methods include, consulting or involving the teachers or their representatives in preparing the text books. Holding discussions with experienced teachers and involving them in text book writing should be a part of the educational policy. They also suggested that the content of books should be in accordance with the changing needs and situations of the society.

This analysis shows that, though they want to participate there is no mechanism to ensure their participation in the making of the syllabus and text books. To a question with regard to the variation in the syllabus from region to region, a large number of them opted for common syllabus for entire state. And about one-third of them opined that the syllabus should vary from place to place so as to suit the regional situations and requirements.

Teachers were also asked to offer their opinion on relevance of teaching methods. Only 28 per cent said that the existing methods are relevant. About 40 per cent stated that the teaching methods are not relevant. The methods, they complain, exclude the students from the learning process. Others said that the teaching methods emphasised in training are such that they cannot be implemented.

Since most of them were trained teachers, the relevance of training is also examined. About 25 per cent opined that it is relevant, but an overwhelming majority thinks that the teaching methods given in the training cannot be implemented in the schools. They said that while a number of methods are imparted in training, schools lack the necessary equipment to implement the methods. They further observed that the practice of those methods is time-consuming and it is not possible to implement them in over-crowded classes.

They were asked to suggest improvements in the training programme. The suggestions include; improvement in the syllabus, integration between the training methods and infrastructure in the school, education of number of students in each class should be reduced and the strength of the teachers be raised and periodicity of the training programme should be more frequent to update the teacher.

When asked to comment on the relevance of existing timings of the school, 75 per cent approved the existing timings, i.e., 10.00 a.m. to 4.00 p.m. with one hour lunch. From the remaining teachers, a few favoured 10.00 a.m. to 4.30 p.m., 9.00 a.m. to 4.00 p.m., 7.00 a.m. to 11.00 a.m. and 8.00 a.m. to 3.00 p.m. with one hour lunch in each case.

Regarding the system of holidays and vacations to the schools, most of the teachers (62%) approved the existing system. They think that the summer vacation becomes necessary as the children cannot bear the sun, and the scarcity of drinking water is assuming alarming dimensions in summer. The rest of the teachers opined that holidays should be in accordance with local needs. They pleaded that a vacation during harvest season would enable the children to be useful to their parents in agricultural operations.

With regard to the examination about 31 per cent of the teachers were satisfied with it. The rest of them were not satisfied. They thought there is need to change the existing system. The change include abolition of non-detention system, introduction of innovative methods to eliminate mal-

In respect of the management of school, all the teachers pleaded for a single management. In the place of Panchayati Raj 80 per cent of the teachers preferred the management of state government. Only 3 per cent preferred Panchayati Raj management, though all the teachers interviewed belonged to Panchayati Raj cadre. The other suggestions include; management to be under a renowned educationist, the schools to be under an autonomous board or a body like university. This indicates that they are against the local management.

When enquired about the reasons for opting government the reasons they told include ; loss of self-respect and dignity in Panchayati Raj, loss of social consciousness and predominance of psychofancy, political pressures from politicians in matters of transfers and promotions, etc. They felt that under state government management these problems would be less acute. To a question about the relevance of education system, only 13 per cent answered in the affirmative but the rest of them felt it is not relevant. When asked for the reasons, they said that there is no relation between what the children study and what they do in life resulting in large scale of unemployment.

When asked to suggest a better system of education, about 50 per cent of the teachers advocated vocational education. They thought that one must be able to acquire some skill to earn their livelihood after the completion. They also suggested that schools should be provided with adequate facilities like building, furniture and teaching aids. A few others suggested that scientific education should be introduced in the schools. There was also a suggestion to resurrect Ashram schools type of education to see that the teaching and learning takes place in a peaceful atmosphere.

To a question about, whether the present education system was helpful to the poor people, about 63 per cent said that it is not at all helpful to the poor. On the contrary they felt it is helpful to the rich and middle class people. About 34 per cent opined that it is helpful to the poor. To gain further insight into the problem, it is attempted to know which type of families were not sending their children to the school. The responses indicate that the economically backward, poor people living at the rock bottom of the society were not sending their children to the school. This includes the Scheduled Caste, Scheduled Tribe and some backward class families like washermen and fishermen. Further probing revealed that the overall poverty conditions account for non-availment of the educational facilities.

VI. Drop-out And Stagnation

Drop-outs and stagnation—getting struck up in the same class—are considered as major constraints in the spread of education in the rural areas. A proper understanding of this phenomenon is necessary. For this purpose the perceptions of the teachers is sought to be analysed.

To the question related to the causes for non-availment of the educational facilities, 66 per cent of the teachers trace the cause to poverty and economic backwardness. The rest of the problems like the needs of the child like food and dressing, child labour, children attending to the household works stem from the roots of poverty. The other cause include ; the unattractive environment of the school, lack of awareness on the part of parents, indifference of the children, etc.

Regarding the problem of drop-outs, and the stages where they drop-out, about 31 per cent stated that generally drop-outs are at the primary stage of studies. About 21 per cent opined that children drop from their studies during their middle school stage. About 31 per cent opined that children drop from their studies in the 5th, 7th and 10th classes, where they have to appear for board examination. It is very difficult in rural areas for the children to pursue their studies once they fail in the examination. Students feel shy of their failure and parent also think that such children are unfit for further studies.

The reasons for drop-out according to the teachers, are the economic backwardness and poverty. The other causes include ; inaccessibility to higher education, failures in examinations, lack of encouragement from parents; non-detention system of school examinations; pressure of household work, unattractive environment of the school; lack of interest on the part of children; child marriages, etc. A part of the explanation that is provided by the practice is that when the children attain the age of 10 or 12, they become fit to do certain physical activities like assisting the parents in agricultural and other caste occupations, doing labour and selling fruits, etc. The parents press them into work which results in dropping them from the education. One teacher opined "loans provided on subsidy basis by the government is causing the problem of drop-outs." With these loans the poor people buy goats, sheep and milch animals. In order to look after these animals, parents are left with no option but withdraw their school-going children from education and entrust them with these responsibilities. They cannot afford to employ another person to look after these animals.

When asked for remedies to the problem of drop-outs and irregular attendance, they suggested certain measures. They include, convincing the parents about the need for education, encouraging the children to continue their studies by creating sufficient interest in them towards education ; compensating for the loss suffered on account of the education by giving regular scholarships, introducing monthly scholarships, establishing more hostels in the villages, providing books and other necessary equipment to the children, introducing compulsory education and vocational education in the schools.

About the non-detention system 94 per cent of the teachers thought that this system should be disbanded and the old detention system should be introduced where every year (in each class) the students used to be examined and detained if they fail to secure minimum marks.

The reasons they gave for opting for a detention system are promotion on the basis of attendanee brings down the quality of education ; it makes the children lazy and indifferent ; teachers are not respected by students and indiscipline among the students is growing, and the 75 per cent attendance has become a farce as everybody manages the attendance by using pressures.

With regard to the other general improvements in the education system, the attitudinal and value pattern of the teacher reveals that they were favourably disposed towards the poorer sections. They want the government to extend all the facilities to the children of the poorer sections. However, they thought that it should be the class and not the caste that should decide the eligibility for help. They also opined that the children of all communities can learn and receive education with equal ability, provided the facilities and proper environment is created. The teachers took a democratic view towards the education of the girls. Although they have some reservation on the existing school education, many of them thought that education is a potential tool for overall development of the society.

This analysis shows that most of the children drop-out at

primary stage and the main reason for drop-out and irregular attendance is poverty and backwardness. The suggestion include better facilities such as hostels, scholarships, free books, etc. There is also a suggestion for reintroduction of detention system. This indicates the emphasis of teachers is on form not on content. On one side they felt that system is irrelevant and they want better results from it on the other.

VIII. Teachers And Their Unions

Here an attempt is made to examine the role of teachers' unions which are considered to be one of the strongest in the organised sector. All the teachers were members of teachers' unions. About 69 per cent were members of Panchayati Raj teachers union. About 28 per cent were members of State Teachers Union and the remaining 3 per cent belong to United Teachers Federation. By and large the teachers belong to the Panchayati Raj teachers union, which is considered to be a big teachers union in the state.

With regard to the role of these unions in solving their problems, only 28 per cent stated that their problems were solved by these unions. About 47 per cent opined that their problems are partially solved by the unions. 19 per cent thought that unions cannot solve their problems. The rest of the teachers felt that union leaders are bothered more about their selfish goals than the problems of the teachers. They indulge in *pyravee* (middlemenship) in settling some of these problems. The teachers were not satisfied with their unions and their effectiveness in solving their problems.

Regarding the contribution of teachers unions to the development of education, 28 per cent of the teachers opined that they played no role in educational development. On the contrary, they felt, unions damaged the cause of education. The unions have been used as ladders by the leaders for their rise to power. 25 per cent of the teachers felt that unions made some contribution to the development of education. About 9 per cent of the teachers opined that they have been useful in solving problems related to transfers and promotion of individual teachers. The unions paid attention to the problems of D.A. and pay scales. There is a small section of the teachers who thought that the unions did raise their voice on certain problems of education and could draw the attention of government.

With regard to the role that these teachers expect the unions to play, the responses were quite interesting. Their expectations include issues such as encouraging parents to send their children to schools, and getting funds from the government for providing better facilities to the children. For this purpose the unions can invite the parents and the officials to attend the conferences on educational problems where the real issues can be discussed. This can be useful in solving the problems of teachers and students. The unions can also take the responsibility to awaken the society. They can organise conferences, training camps for teachers and make them realise their duties. They can draw the attention of the government to the deficiencies in text-books, syllabus and facilities in the schools.

Summing-up

Since teachers constitute an important component of educational administration, an attempt is made to examine their problems and perceptions. An analysis of their social background indicates that most of them are from backward castes with reasonable academic qualifications and trained skills. While their origins are in rural areas, they received their education in urban areas. They categorised themselves largely as middle class. The background is largely in conformity with the rural educational administration.

The perceptions of the teachers with regard to the infrastructure reveals and confirms the earlier finding that the infrastructure is quite inadequate. Some of the schools do not have even full complement of the teachers. They resented the existing conditions and facilities and felt that it is not conducive for sound education. Even in those cases where the facilities are extended, they thought it is neither given in sufficient quantity nor in time.

Regarding the teacher-community relations, there is a general feeling of alienation from students and village people.

In the case of students, the teachers have come to feel that they do not enjoy their respect and they perceive growing indiscipline among the students. In the case of villagers, the school-village interaction is rare. They also felt that the elite have no respect for the teachers. The parental committees, which are intended to provide a forum for interaction have become ornamental.

With regard to the problems of teachers such as appointment, promotion, transfers, retirement, housing, etc., the responses indicate the general dissatisfaction with the existing educational management. In respect of recruitment they preferred government management to Panchayati Raj control. In the case of transfers they felt that the norms are not uniformally applied. In matters of promotion many of them thought that the gap is too wide and the basis of promotion not sound. They also complained about their facilities like housing in the villages.

About the relevance of present education, they do not seem to have a clear-cut idea. However, livelihood, awareness and knowledge are stated to be the objectives of education. About the relevance of books, the teachers opined that the learning and education should be relevant to the future life of the children. In the place of the present education they pleaded for technical and vocational education. As the present practice does not include the teachers' participation in preparation of the text-books, they pleaded for greater involvement of the teachers in this process. The teachers also think that the teaching methods and training of the teachers are neither realistic nor academically sound. On the whole they consider the present education not relevant to social needs nor give a career to the boys and girls.

They broadly agree that present education is not helpful and accessible to rural poor. They trace poverty and backward-n ess as root causes for non-availment of the existing educational facilities and large scale drop-outs. Absence of facilities and unattractive conditions in the school aggravated the problem further.

Regarding the role of teachers unions, they are largely dissatisfied. They expect the unions to play a greater role than what they are doing presently. They suggested that unions can take upon the responsibility of ensuring better rapport between the teacher and the government on one hand and the teacher and the community in general on the other.

The silverlining in the whole analysis is the general value disposition of these teachers. They share broadly the democratic values and think that education should be extended to all the sections and more so to the rural poor. They also think that right type of education can play a crucial role in the development of the society. Except for this brighter side, in all respects the analysis indicates the gloomy side of rural educational development.

REFERENCES

1. *Report of Indian Education Commission, 1954-66, op. cit*, p. 46
2. J.P. Naik, *Policy and Performance in Indian Education*, 1947-74, *op. cit.*, p. 66
3. In the banking concept, education becomes an act of depositing. in which the students are the depositories and teacher is the depositor. 'Instead of communicating, the teacher issues communiques and 'makes deposits'. Which the students paiently receive memorize and repeat. This is the 'banking' concept of education, in which the scope of action allowed to the students extends only as far as receiving, filling, and storing deposits'. Here 'the relationship involves a narrating subjects (the teacher) and patient, listening objects (the students). See Paulo Freire, *Pedagogy of the Oppressed, op. cit.*, p. 45-46
4. In the words of Bertrand Russel, 'the old idea of discipline was simple. A child or boy was ordered to do something he disliked, or abstaln from something he liked. When he disobeyed he suffered physical chastisement, or, in extreme cases, solitary confinement on bread and water'—See Bertrand Russel, *On Education*, Unwin Books. London, 1971, p. 21

5

Problems and Perceptions of Students

Students constitutes the heart of the education system. They are the most affected segment by both the strength and weakness of the education system. Although in terms of age they may not be adults, yet their feelings would provide an insight into the working of the rural educational administration. For this purpose the sample is drawn from the students of IX and X classes of the secondary school. The socio-economic profile of the students is as follows :—

TABLE 5.1

Educational Levels Of Students

Educational Level	Girls	Boys	Total
Class IX	5 (11.91) (5.88)	37 (88.09) (43.53)	42 (10.00) (49.41)
Class X	6 (13.95) (7.06)	37 (88.05) (43.53)	43 (100.00) (50.59)
Total	11 (12.94)	74 (87.06)	85 (100.00)

Note : Figures in brackets indicate percentages to the totals

The Table 5.1 reveals that out of 85 student respondents in the study, 42 (49.41) belong to class IX, and 43 (50.59) to class X. There were 11 (12.94) girl students of which 5 (5.88) belong to class IX and 6(7.06) to class X. There were 74(87.06) boys, of which 37 (43.53) belong to class IX and another 37 (43.53) to class X. Since the students come from IX and X class all of them were teenagers.

TABLE 5.2

Caste Background Of Students

Caste	Frequency	Percentage
F.C.	28	32.94
B.C.	50	58.82
S.C.	7	8 24
Total	85	100.00

The caste background of the students (Table 5.2) shows that 28 (32.94) of them come from forward castes—predominantly from Reddy Caste—and others come from Komati (Merchant) and Muslim communities. There were 50 (58.82) students belonging to backward castes, which include Mudiraj (Fishing), Padmashali (Weaving), and Gouda (Taddy Tapping) communities and the others from 'Dudekula', Telaga (a farming community) Are Marata (also a farming community), Vadla (Carpentry), Golla (Shepherd), Perika (Weavers of Jute), Kummari (Pottery) and Ousula (Goldsmith) communities. The remaining 7 (8.24) students belong to the Scheduled Caste (Harijan) community. Significantly, there were no Scheduled Tribes students in the class IX and class X in the school under study.

The parental occupation revealed that slightly less than half (45.88) of their parents live on agriculture and these parents are mostly drawn from forward castes and a few of them belong to backward class community. About 4.7 per cent parents live on weaving, 8.24 per cent on tadday tapping, 4.7 per cent on carpentry, 2.35 per cent on fishing, 1.18 per cent work as *mestri* (supervising construction works), and another 1.18 are Goldsmiths. Parents of all these respondents live on their traditional caste based occupations which are categorised

TABLE 5.3

Parental Occupations Of Students

Caste	Agriculture	Weaving	Toddy tapp-ing	Labour	Carpen-try	Fishing	RMP Doctor	Petty Hotel	Gold Smith	Others	Total
F.C.	20(71.43)	—	—	1(3.57)	—	—	—	—	—	7(25.00)	28(100.00 (32.94
B.C.	15(30.00)	4(8.00)	7(14.00)	2(4 00)	4(8.00)	2(4.00)	1(2.00)	2(4.00)	11(22.00)		50(100.00) (58.82)
S.C.	4(57.14)	—	—	2(28.57)	—	—	—	—	—	1(14.29)	7(100.00) (8.24)
Total	39(45.88)	4(4.7)	7(8.24)	5(5.88)	4(4.70)	2(2.35)	2(3 35)	1(1.18)	2(2.36)	19(22.33)	85(100.00)

as backward. 2.35 per cent parents work as R.M.P. doctors, 1.18 per cent each live on petty hotel business, pan shop and tailoring. From the remaining sample, parents include kirana shopkeeper, lorry drivers, government employees, teachers, petty traders such as fruit-vendors, ice-cream sellers, petty leather traders, etc. The categories of government employees include police constables, village development officers, lower division clerks, etc. (See Table 5.3)

The level of parental education of the students indicates that as many as 78.67 per cent of their mothers were illiterates, 16.46 per cent were educated upto primary levels, only 2.35 per cent of them completed middle or high school education. While most of the educated mothers belong to forward castes or backward class communities, there is only one educated mother from the Scheduled Caste community (see Table 5.4).

TABLE 5.4

Parental Education Of Students

	FC	BC	SC	Total
Mothers's Education				
i. Illiterate	20(71.43)	41(82 00)	6(85.71)	67
ii. Primary	6(21.43)	7(14.00)	1(14.29)	14
iii. Middle	1(3.57)	1(2.00)	—	2
iv. Secondary	1(3.57)	1(2.00)	—	2
Total	28(32.94)	50(58.82)	7(8.24)	85
Father's Education				
i. Illiterate	10(35.71)	22(44.00)	4(57.14)	36
ii. Primary	8(28.57)	16(32.00)	2(42.86)	27
iii. Middle	4(14.28)	6(12.00)	—	10
iv. Secondary	4(14.28)	2(4.00)	—	6
v. Inter/PUC	1(3.57)	1(2.00)	—	2
vi. Graduation	1(3.57)	3(6.00)	—	4
Total	28(32.94)	50(58.82)	7(8.24)	85

The education of fathers is some what better than that of mothers There were 41.18 per cent illiterate fathers, most of them come from backward classes and the Scheduled Caste communities. There were 58.82 per cent literates among the fathers. 31.76 per cent fathers are educated upto primary level, 11.76 per cent upto middle school level, 7.05 per cent upto high school level. Only 2.35 per cent belonging to forward castes and a few backward class communities are educated upto Intermediate or P.U.C. levels, and 4.70 per cent belonging to forward caste and backward class communities were educated upto graduation.

Regarding the details about their place of education, 37.64 per cent of the student respondents studied in their own village right from the beginning. 2.36 per cent spent their childhood in urban areas, i.e., headquarters of the district. The remaining majority were going outside their villages right from their early childhood for the purpose of education.

TABLE 5.5

Place of Students-Natives and Outsiders

Native Place	Frequency	Percentage
Natives of the village	35	41.18
Outsiders	50	58.82
Total	85	100.00

When enquired about their native place, of the total sample of 85 students only 41.18 per cent were the natives of Kur—the village under study. The other students come from fourteen surrounding villages. It means the school in 'Kur', in addition to meeting the local needs, has to meet the demands of 14 other villages. The distance of these villages ranges from one kilometre to ten kilometres.

From 58.82 per cent of the outside students, 11.76 per cent stay in 'Kur' village itself with either their relatives or in rented houses. The remaining 47.06 per cent students commute every day from their native villages to the 'Kur' village to attend to the classes.

Of this 47.06 per cent students who commute daily from their villages, 14.12 per cent commute by bicycles and 32.94 per cent by walk. This shows that the children from outside the village studying in secondary school out-number the children of the native village. Since they cannot afford to stay in the village where the school is located, they have to commute the distance. Since all of them cannot afford to buy a bicycle, they had to walk every day one kilometre to ten kilometres up and one kilometre to ten kilometres down. Since all the villages are not connected even with a fair weather road and bus, they cannot even come by bus. In those case where there are bus facilities, they cannot afford to travel by bus every day. This brings out the pangs that a rural student has to undergo to complete his secondary school education, not to think of higher education.

Of the total students who commute daily, half of them have a fair weather road either to walk or to come by bicycle. The remaining are made to walk either on a muddy road or on a pedestrain path. An examination into the difficulties faced by the students in commuting every day revealed the tremendous suffering that they undergo in the process. The students lamented that during the summer season they have to bear the brunt of the sun and during the rainy season they have to walk in the mud and water. Some times they get struck up because of the over-flowing streams. One cannot use bicycles in such conditions. Most of the students complained that their legs ache in the evenings due to long walk or cycling. They said that due to rain and sun they get delayed either in reaching the school or home.

The following comments made by the students sharply focus the problem ; One student said, 'In the early morning we have to work in our fields (agriculture) and immediately rush to the school on foot. Some times we get delayed to the school'. Another student said, 'If it rains, cycle is not useful, then we walk to the school in mud and water. Some times it becomes difficult to cross the over-flowing streams. In the process we get delayed to the school'. The third said, 'In the rainy season, in order to carefully cut across our way through the mud and stream, we have to start much earlier in the morning, i.e., at 8.30 a.m. to reach the school at 10.00 a m.' The fourth observed, 'we have to walk for one-and-half hours in the morning and one-and-half hours in the evening to reach the school and back home. To cut short the distance we take to paths which are muddy and thorny. In the summer, we rest under the trees while on our way back home'. The fifth said, 'I have to walk 12 kilometres (up and down) a day. We have to leave home at 8.00 a.m. and return at 5.00 p.m.' Yet another student said, 'I have to cycle 20 kilometres (up and down) a day of which 14 kilometres is muddy road and 6 kilometres fair weather road. This has to be done with a cycle that constantly gives trouble'. These were some of the comments and observations made by the students. This unfolds difficulties that they have to put up in pursuing their education.

TABLE 5.6

The way the Students Spend Their Leisure and Vacation

Response	Frequency	Percentage
Work in own agricultural fields	32	37.65
Work as daily wage labourer	24	28.24
Work in caste occupation	6	7.06
Others	23	27.05
Total	85	100.00

About the way they spend their leisure and vacation, more than half of the students reported that they work during the vacation. Thirty-eight per cent of them reported that they work in their own agricultural fields, 28.24 per cent work as daily wage labourers. A few students said that they sell ice-cream, collect milk for dairy farm, assist their fathers in caste occupations, work in the poultry farm, make beedies, and cycle repairs, etc. The general impression that the students in India do not work while learning is not largely true in the rural areas. (Table 5.6).

(a) Students Perceptions an Infrastructure

Here an attempt is made to examine the perceptions of the students about the infrastructural facilities. For this purpose they were asked about the adequacy of class-rooms and teachers. An overwhelming number of the students were found satisfied with the existing situation. A few students reported that they have no teachers for scout, crafts and Hindi.

Since the sample is drawn from the secondary school, the problems that crops up in the primary and upper primary are noticed.

To the questions about the attendance of teachers, 75 per cent of the students reported that the teachers come regularly and 25 per cent said that the teachers are irregular. Those who said that the teachers come late said that it is because they stay outside the village (i.e. in town). They also complained that most of the teachers while away their time and let off the classes.

With regard to furniture and library, most of the students expressed their satisfaction. However, they expressed the difficulties in getting the books from the library. In the case of text-books distribution also quite a large number of them made no complaint. However, one-fourth of the students reported that they received the books very late. A few students said that they did not get mathematics books till the end of the academic year.

TABLE 5.7

Particulars of Students Getting Scholarships

Caste	Did not get anything	Got Rs. 40—90	Total
F.C.	28(100.00)	—	28(100.00)
B.C.	24(48.00)	26(52.00)	50(100.00)
S.C.	1(14.28)	6(85.00)	7(100.00)
Total	53(62.35)	32(37.65)	85(100.00)

About the free aid from the government 82 23 per cent reported that they did not recieve any benefit. The remaining (11.77) students mostly from the Scheduled Castes stated that they got text books free of cost. About the scholarships also, 62 per cent of the students were not recipients of any scholarships. 38 per cent got scholarships ranging from Rs. 45 to Rs. 90 per annum. From those who got scholarships a large majority were from the weaker sections. About 50 per cent from the backward castes and almost all the students from the Scheduled Castes were recipients of the scholarships.

TABLE 5.8

Students Perception on Adequacy of Facilities

Facilities	Adequate	Inadequate	Total
Laboratory	52 (61.18)	33 (38.82)	85
Library	61 (71.76)	24 (28.24)	85
Toilets	—	85 (100.00)	85
Drinking Water	14 (16.47)	71 (83.53)	85

With regard to the laboratory facilities, though all the students agreed that a laboratory exists in their school, 38.83 per cent students said that it is not adequately equipped. Further probing indicates that more than half (51.77) of the students have not had the benefit of the laboratory. The students held that the teachers themselves complain that there is no equipment and there are instances when teachers have shown the broken instruments to the students and expressed their helplessness. Even the students who offered favourable comments on other aspects of the school expressed their dissatisfaction with the working of the laboratory.

About a few basic facilities like toilets and drinking water, the students are found thoroughly dissatisfied. They enumerated a number of difficulties in this regard. The girl students are found more distressed about the absence of toilet facilities. The students—both boys and girls—were unanimous in their bitter reactions about the absence of a facility like drinking water. They narrated the difficulty in getting a glass of water from some of the neighbouring houses who not only refuse water but make no secret of their annoyance. The problem is felt more acutely by the students coming from outside the village. This problem assumes alarming dimensions partly due to scarcity of water in the village.

Regarding their opinion on games and sports, all the students stated that there are play grounds and a games teacher. Regarding games material 32 per cent of the students reported that they do not have proper games material to play. The others said that they have the facilities to play kabadi, khoko, volley ball, badminton etc.

TABLE 5.9

Participation of Students in Games, NCC and Scouts

Response	Frequency	Percentage
Do not participate	74	87.06
Participate	11	12.94
Total	85	100.00

To a direct question whether they avail the facilities such as games, NCC, Scout, most of the students are found to be non-participants. The main reason appears to be the distance between the school and the village. This knocks away all their leisure time. On holidays they have pressure of their household duties or agricultural operations. Thus, there is no scope for their personality development through the extra-curricular activites.

(b) Students' Views on Teacher-Students Relations

As students have direct relations and constant interaction with the teachers, here an attempt is made to examine the emerging pattern of relations between the student and the teacher as perceived by the students. An understanding and cordial relations between the students and the teachers can provide a stimulus for the learning process. At the outset they were asked about the treatment they get from the teachers a large majority of them commented favourably about it.

About the punishment system they were asked whether their teachers cane them, a majority (67.08) said that they do not. About 33 per cent reported such type of punishment. When asked for the causes for punishment, the students did not make any charges or accusations against any teacher. Most of them said that it is largely on account of their own negligence, bad performance in studies, failure to answer questions. On the whole they traced the cause for punishment to their own failings.

The students were asked to rate their teachers in order of their liking for them. About 36 per cent expressed their liking for Mr. F followed by Mr. M, Mr. N, Mr. C, Mr. O and a few others. The reasons upper most in students' mind for liking a teacher are : the willingness of the teachers to mix-up with the students informally and treat students as brothers and sons, explaining difficult lessons, have no hesitation to repeat the lessons and answer the questions, only teachers with such qualities are considered as good teachers. According to them as persons the teachers require to have the following qualities ; a good person should evince constant interest, he should guide and shape the students as good citizens, inculcate discipline among the students, should be warm and affectionate, should not discriminate the students on caste and other considerations. Interestingly, those teachers who are categorised as 'good' persons are also found to be effective teachers.

An enquiry into good teaching revealed that the students like teaching with illustrations and support of maps and experiments to the lesson. They also said that good teachers explain each and every word very clearly. To avoid boredom to the students, good teachers crack jokes now and then in the course of teaching. The students observed that good teachers are found always willing to explain and they do not mind even when the students go to their houses and bother them. The qualities of a good teacher that emerges from the above description are ; proper teaching techniques, clear exposition, humourous approach and accessibility to the students.

TABLE 5.10

Subjects that are Liked by the Students

Subjects	Frequency	Percentage
Mathematics	22	25.88
Telugu	16	18.82
General Science	14	16.47
Social Studies	8	9.41
English	8	9.41
Hindi	2	2.35
Others (liked more than one subject)	15	17.65

To a question about the subjects they like, about 26 per cent liked Mathematics 16 per cent General Science 19 per cent Telugu and 9 per cent each Social Studies and English. The table 5.10 also shows the least liked subject was Hindi (2.35). Further probing revealed that it is the teacher and usefulness of the subject that makes a subject attractive. This was confirmed from the responses of the students to a question on their choice of good teachers. The teacher in Mathematics Mr. R was the most liked one followed by the teacher in Telugu Mr. M and General Science Mr. N. There was a strong coincidence between a good teacher and a good person and an interesting subject.

(c) Students Views on Problems of Education

Here an attempt is made to elicit the students point of view on problems of present education. In the first place, they were asked about the uses of education. This can provide a fair idea about their perceptions. 55.29 per cent of the students thought that education imparts social awareness, knowledge and helps in getting employment. They also felt that education would help them in becoming doctors, mechanics, drivers, teachers, police officers, conductors, etc. They also mentioned that it enables them to read bus boards, differentiate quality goods from duplicate, they can earn money with the help of education. A few said that one can stand on his own legs because of education. 22.35 per cent students also said that education is useful for betterment of the nation as well as individual. A few of them also felt that they can understand the developments both at the national and international levels because of education. About 8 per cent said that education increases the political awareness and gives the ability to

TABLE 5.11

Students Perception of Reasons for Illiteracy

Reasons	Frequency	Percentage
Poverty and economic difficulties	26	30.59
Agriculture and household works	23	27.06
Working as contract labour	6	7.06
Working as daily wage labourer	5	6.88
Others	25	29.40
Total	85	100.00

exercise the vote properly. A few students also stated that it can help them to grow more disciplined, responsible and attain higher goals in life. A few girl students said that education enables them to help the illiterates and also question the injustice being inflicted on women.

In order to elicit the responses of the students on problems of illiteracy among their counterparts in the villages, they were asked a question in this regard. About 90 per cent of the students reported that all the boys and girls o· their age were not going to the school. To another question about the reasons for this trend, about 31 per cent of the students traced it to poverty and economic difficulties (See Table 5.11). About 27 per cent of the students stated that the agricultural work and household activities account for the children remaining outside the school system. About 7 per cent of them said that the children are working as contracted labour (jeetam) to earn livelihood which prevent them going to school. A few others also said that they work as daily wage labour. Others said that irregular functioning of the school is also partly responsible for this trend. This, most of the students traced the cause for illiteracy to poverty in rural areas.

TABLE 5.12

Students Perception of Reasons for Drop-Outs

Reasons	Frequency	Percentage
Agricultural works	20	23.53
Economic difficulties	16	18.83
Child marriage	13	15.29
Others	36	42.35
Total	85	100.00

Regarding the problem of drop-outs, as shown in the Table 5.12, almost all the students stated that there is incidence of drop-outs. When enquired about the reasons for drop-outs, 24 per cent said agricultural works as the main cause. About 19 per cent traced it to economic difficulties. About 15 per cent said child marriage as the cause for drop-outs. The other reasons mentioned by the students includes ; ill-health, lack of parental interest in education, children engaged in contract labour, death of parents, pressure of household occupational works and lack of high schools in all the villages.

With regard to suitability of the present pattern of education they were asked certain questions. In respect of present pattern of vacation and holidays 82.3 pre cent preferred the existing arrangement, i.e., vacation during the summer. They felt that it is difficult to study during the summer. There were also suggestions for vacations during the rainy or winter season. Those who preferred rainy season maintained that it is difficult to reach the school during this season.

With regard to the existing examination system, an overwhelming number of students did not find anything wrong with it. A few of them did suggest open book system or objective type of examination. About the school timings also 90 per cent of them preferred existing timings, i.e., 10.00 a.m. to 4.00 p.m.

About improvements in existing education and its contents, about 37 per cent could not answer. 35.5 per cent suggested training in some trade like carpentry, workshop training, electrical engineering, tailoring, typewriting drawing, poultry, embroidary, crafts, etc. About 12 per cent suggested introdution of technical education. A few students said that the standards of existing education are quite high and are not within the reach of an average student. Therefore, they pleaded for reduction in the standards There was also a suggestion for greater concentration on Telugu, instead of a foreign language like English. Updating the syllabus was another suggestion made by the students.

About their choice of courses, 15 per cent said that they would study upto intermediate, 21 per cent opted for polytechnic education, 7 per cent preferred engineering course, 4 per cent wanted to undergo teacher training course, 12 per cent preferred ITI, 6 per cent wanted jobs after completing school education, 16.43 per cent were anxious to study medicine. Remaining preferred to study upto their B.A. or M.A. LL.B. 7 per cent left it to parental choice. A few wanted to take caste occupation after school education. This analysis shows, that they were also alive to the economic difficulties. The rural students were conscious of their future studies.

TABLE 5.13

Students Choice of Courses After School Education

Choice	Frequency	Percentage
Intermediate	13	15.29
Polytechnic	18	21.18
I.T.I.	10	11.76
Engineering	6	7.06
Teacher Training	3	3.53
Medicine	14	16.43
M.A. or LL.B.	5	5.88
Employment	5	5.88
Caste Occupation	5	5.88
It depends on parents	6	7.06
Total	85	100.00

To the question whether they would pursue their higher studies, a large majority of them answered in the affirmative and also thought that their parents will not have much difficulty in sending them for higher education. However, about 39 per cent of the students belonging to the backward and Scheduled Castes were not hopeful of pursuing the studies and thought that their parents would not be able to send them for higher education. They were alive to the economic problems in which their parents are caught up. They consider that they can be of some help to their parents in agricultural and other household operations. Thus, the economic background shaping the attitudes and ambitions of the students is quite obvious in the response pattern.

Summing-Up

An analysis of problems and perceptions of rural students presents a different dimension of educational administration. The major problem seems to be the distance. As the students come from different and far off villages, they had to commute from one kilometre to ten kilometres. They expressed several difficulties in walking the long distances. This obviously knocks away their leisure and they get so tired that they cannot concentrate on their studies, nor can participate in extra curricular activities like games, NCC and Scout. Contrary to the general belief that students do not earn while learning and lack dignity of labour, it is found that quite a number of students participate in agricultural operations and assist the parents in a number of activities. A few students from poorer families do take up even daily wage labour during the vacation.

With regard to the school timings, and the present scheme of vacation, a large number of them were in favour of the existing arrangement. In respect of facilities while the students largely reported that do have certain facilities in their school, they had complaints in matters of library, laboratory, toilets and drinking water. The responses indicate that these facilities did not exist or they were scanty. While the Scheduled Caste students and a few from the backward castes were getting the scholarships, a large majority were not covered by any of these schemes.

In respect of the teacher-student relations, the responses reveal that they were reasonably impressive. There was not much of caning and punishment. It is interesting to note that the students were found interested in those subjects which are taught well. The teachers of those subjects were also warm and informal. The students appreciate the teachers using maps and humour while teaching. With regard to their future plans, most of them proposed to study some technical short-term courses, although about one fourth of them proposed to study professional courses like engineering and medicine. Most of them were conscious of their economic limitations and limited opportunities to pursue higher education.

The students pointed out poverty and economic backwardness as the principal causes for illiteracy in the villages. This is the reason, according to them, that accounts for a number of boys from their age group remaining outside the school or drop-out in the middle. A few responses indicate that the social practices like early marriage, pressure of work either in the house or in the field also account for this phenomenon.

The socio-economic profile of students indicate that only 45 per cent of them come from the agricultural background.

This obviously excludes a large number of children from agricultural labour households. There were only 6 per cent of the children from the labour households. Interestingly, 23 per cent of the children belong to the families dependent on traditional caste occupations. About one third of the children come from the families largeiy belonging to the formal sector or those working in the modern professions. The rest of the children arc kept outside the school system. It is this factor that explains the difficulties inherent in the universalisation of education in the rural sector. And those who are in the school system feel handicapped and the overall system is not in a position for the development of the personality or skills of the rural youth.

6

Attitudes and Perceptions of Parents and Village Elite

In this chapter, the attitudes and perceptions of parents and elite towards rural education are examined. The parents and elite constitute a crucial variable in rural educational system. The main purpose of the chapter is to examine the perceptions of these groups about conduciveness of the educational system and the problems it is facing to attain the goal of universal education. For this purpose an attempt is made to elicit the opinion of 205 parents, 50 village elite drawn from the villages where the schools included in this study are located.

I. Attitudes of Parents Towards Rural Education

An examination of attitudes of the parents on education is very important. For in the rural situation it is the parental decision that determines the 'fact' of the child. If the parents take a favourable attitude towards education it can work as a catalyst. An unfavourable attitude can become a constraint on the goal of the universalisatton of education.

The parents of the study mostly come from Backward Castes like Mudiraj (Fishing Community), Gouda (Toddy Tapping), Padmasali (Weaving), Telega (Farming), Golla (Shephered) and other service castes like Chakali (Washerman), Mangali (Barber) Vadla (Carpenter), Kummari (Pottery), Kammari (Blacksmith) etc., castes. The remaining come from Forward Castes like Reddy, Komati and Brahmin. The sample also includes respondents from Scheduled Caste Community. Very few come from Erukalu, a Scheduled Tribe Community. A large number of parents come from either poor class or from middle class. A very few come from rich class. Most of the rich belong to the Forward Castes. While majority of these respondents depend on agriculture, others depend on caste occupations or physical labour. Majority of them were illiterates and a few were educated upto primary and high school levels (see Table 6.1, 6.2, 6.3)

At the outset the enquiry reveals that more than 90 per cent of the parents were having school going children. But some of the parents were not sending all the children to the school, of course in most of the children not sent to the school happen to be girls.

Table 6.4 reveals that 89.43 per cent, 66.66 per cent and 31.82 per cent of parents of 'Kur', 'Konda' and 'Peta' villages respectively were sending their children to the local school. As there is a high school in 'Kur' village, only 8.13 per cent of the respondents were sending their children to the other villages and cities. 'Konda' village where there is an upper primary school about 25 per cent of the parents were sending their children to the other villages for study purposes. From 'Peta' village where there was a single-teacher school, as many as 59.09 per eent of the parents were compelled to send their children to the other villages for studies including primary education. However some parents were not sending their children to any school. For those who attend the schools in other villages the distance from native village ranges from 2 km. to 25 km. Most of the children of the respondents of 'Kur' village who study in other villages study at the district headquarters and stay there. A few commute by R.T.C. bus every day. In case of Konda village most of the children have to go to 'Kuri' village which is 5 km. away from 'Konda' or to the district headquarters (15 km.). A few children stay in the other villages and a few commute by bus daily. The bulk

TABLE 6.1

Caste and Class Background of Parents

Caste/Class	F.C.	B.C.	S.C.	S.T.	Total
Rich	8 (80.00)	2 (20.00)	—	—	10 (100.00) (4.88)
Middle	26 (29.55)	57 (64.77)	5 (5.68)	—	88 (100.00) (42.93)
Poor	17 (15.89)	60 (56.07)	26 (24.30)	4 (3.74)	107 (100.00) (52.19)
Total	51 (24.88)	119 (58.05)	31 (15.12)	4 (1.95)	205 (100.00)

of the children from 'Peta' village have been studying in other villages and walk every day from 2 km. (Konda village) to 4 km. (another village). The small children have to trek a distance of 4 km. to 8 km. every day resulting in fatigue and ill-health.

TABLE 6.2

Occupation of Parents

Occupation	Frequency	Percentage
Agriculture	68	33.17
Daily wage and contract labour	36	17.56
Toddy tapping	16	7.80
Weaving	11	5.36
Sheep and cattle rearing	10	4.87
Fishing	9	4.39
Washermen	8	3.90
Tailoring	5	2.43
Petty trading	5	2.43
Employment	5	2.43
Construction supervision	4	1.95
Business	4	1.95
Carpentry	3	1.46
Hair cutting	3	1.46
Pottery	2	0.97
Goldsmith and balacksmith	2	0.97
Others	14	0.83
Total	205	100.00

An attempt is made to know the problems faced by the parents in sending their children to the school. 20 per cent of the parents mostly belonging to FCs and BCs of rich, and middle classes, faced no problems in sending their children to the school. The others reported economic difficulties in sending the children to school is causing inconvenience in the agricultural operations. They felt it is difficult to run agriculture without their children's help. Some of them reported that due to poverty they cannot afford clothes, fee and books to

TABLE 6.3

Educational Levels of Parents

Education	Frequency	Percentage
Illiterate	103	50.24
Primary	60	29.27
Secondary	39	19.03
Intermediate or PUC	2	0.98
Graduation	1	0.49
Total	205	100.00

the school going children. There is also the problem of infants at home. The grown up children are made to take care of these infants. A few other parents stated that as their children do not study well, they arranged for private tuitions causing a burden on the domestic budget. Some of the parents reported that they were even borrowing the money to meet the children's educational expenditure. Four parents said that they face the problem in sending the children to outside the village as the facilities do not exist in their own village.

With regard to the expenditure incurred by the parents in educating their children, about 28 per cent of the respondents reported (Table 6.5) that it has been between Rs. 100 to 200 per annum. 11.22 per cent incur between Rs. 201-300 per annum, 20.49 per cent spend between Rs. 301-500, 7.80 per cent spend Rs. 501-700, about 11 per cent spend Rs. 701-1000. There were 7.32 per cent of the parents who spend Rs. 1000 to 1500. A few parents reported that it is as high as Rs. 1500 to 2000 per annum.

When asked about the reasons for sending their children to the school, almost all the parents stated that they were doing it with a hope that they would get job and settle down. They also thought that education would make them clever and improve their awareness about the socio-economic conditions. This they felt would help the children to carve a better life for themselves.

TABLE 6.4

Children of Respondents Studying in Local and Other Schools

Village	Studying in local school	Studying in outside school	No child is going to schcol at present	Total
Kur	110 (89.43)	10 (8.13)	3 (2.44)	123 (100.00
Konda	40 (66.66)	15 (25.00)	5 (8.34)	60 (100.00)
Peta	7 (31.82)	13 (59.09)	2 (9.09)	22 (100.00)
Total	157 (76.59)	38 (18.54)	10 (4.87)	205 (100.00)

TABLE 6.5

Expenditure of Parents on their Children's Education

Expenditure (Rs. per annum)	Frequency	Percentage
100 to 200	58	28.29
201 to 300	23	11.22
301 to 500	42	20.49
501 to 700	16	7.80
701 to 1000	23	11.22
1001 to 1500	15	7.32
1501 to 2000	18	8.78
Not sending children to school	10	4.87
Total	205	100.00

A. Parents Attitude towards Drop-out Children

The problem of drop-out is a serious impediment in the spread of education in rural areas. It is in this context, an attempt is made to examine the perceptions towards this issue. Out of 205 total respondents, 148 (72.19) parents were not having drop-out children in their homes. The reason for not having many drop-outs[1] among the better off forward caste families has been economic status and their interest in children's education. The reasons for low drop outs among S.C. and S.T. families has been partly due to the fact that they were sending the children for the first time and partly the enrolment from these families itself was quite limited. The phenomenon of drop-outs occurs in the poor, lower middle class and Scheduled Caste families. The lower middle classes have a desire to educate the children but were economically handicapped. It is for this reason the incidence of drop-outs has been noticed among these families.

Table 6.6 reveals that out of 57 parents who were having drop-outs, as many as 23 (40.35) parents stated that their children dropped out because of economic difficulties, 3 (5.26) said due to pressure of work at home, 4 (7.01) said because of early marriage. 5 (8.77) said due to beatings of the teachers, 10 (17.54) said because of agricultural work. Other reasons include looking after the infants and guarding

TABLE 6.6

Reasons for Drop-outs

Reasons	Frequency	Percentage
Economic difficulties	23	40.35
Pressure of work at home	3	5.26
Early marriage	4	7.02
Beating of the teacher	5	8.77
Agricultural works	10	17.54
Others	12	21.05
Total	57	100.00

the home and cannot afford to engage the labour for agricultural operations. On the whole poverty appears to be the dominant cause.

An examination of the stage at which their children became drop-outs, out of the 57 respondents 22 (38.60) reported that their children dropped out in class I or II. From these twenty two drop-outs thirteen were male and 9 female. 16(28.07) parents reported that their children dropped in class III or class V. Of this sixteen, eight were male and other eight were female. 9 (15.79) parents said that their children dropped at VI or VII class, of which seven were male and two were female. Another 10 (17.54) respondents reported that their children dropped in class X, of which eight were male and two female. This analysis shows that out of 57 parents who had drop-outs 36 were having male drop-outs. The incidence of male drop-outs is higher as it is only male children who are sent to the school and not female children. Therefore, the problem of drop-outs does not arise in the case of female children.

When probed into the occupational particulars of the drop-outs, out of 57 respondents twelve (21.05) said that their children were working in their own fields, eight (14.03) said that their children were working as hired labour or engaged themselves in beedi making activity, another five (8.77) said that children were working as contracted labourers (Jeetam) in the fields of the rich, six (10.52) said their children were involved in household activities such as looking small babies guarding the home whenever parents are out, fetching water for family use etc. Four (7.01) respondents said that their children were working in petty jobs such as lorry cleaner, sales boy etc., five (8.77) said their children were engaged in their traditional occupations such as toddy tapping, carpentry etc. In ten cases (17.54) the girls got married and left the education. A few others reported that their children were engaged in tailoring, selling of seasonal fruits, ice-creams etc.

To a question whether anybody attempted to persuade them to send the drop-outs back to the school, except one respondent, none answered in the affirmative. This shows how the question of drop-outs is totally ignored.

B. Parental Attitudes Towards Non-school Going Children

Out of the total 205 parents 127 (61.95) parents do not belong to this category. The number of parents who have illiterate children[2] is 78 (38.05) and most of them come from B.C., S.C., and S.T., communities of poor and lower middle class.

An attempt is also made to examine the causes for not sending the children to the school. Out of 78 families as many as 42 (53.85) parents stated indebtedness as the main cause. Others stated reasons such as household activities, looking after the infant children, assistance in agricultural operations and assistance in caste professions.

Some of the following comments from parents put the issue in a sharper focus. "Lack of educational climate in the house, and educating girls is not an easy thing in these days". "Because of my incapability to clear the debts and invest in the education of children, I kept him with a landowner as contract labourer (Jeetam),'. "I have a small agricultural holding, I cannot send all the children to school with the meagre income I get from agriculture". "We never thought of schooling a child; all our children joined as contract labourers (Jeetam) eversince they attained the age of eight'; "She will be assisting her mother at home, even if we educate her, it is not possible to get a suitable (educated) husband to her". "We have four goats, he (child) looks after them every day", "Ours is a poor family, if we and he (child) together go for labour we get something to eat". 'I am already sending two children to school. That is why I am keeping the third one at home to assist me in agriculture." These are some of the comments made by the parents, which provide an explanation as to why parents do not send their children to the school.

An examination of the nature of work that the non-school going children carry out indicates the following pattern. The works include household activities like fetching water, sweeping the house, baby sitting, guarding the home and assisting the mother in kitchen; undertaking own agricultural activities like watering the crops, ploughdg, weeding cattle and sheep rearing, etc. In addition, a few children were working as 'Jeethagandlu' (contracted labourers for a year) which involves attending of all agricultural activities. A few of them were working on daily wage basis in agricultural fields or in tiles factory. There were instances where they were assisting parents in carrying out the work associated with traditional caste occupations.

TABLE 6.7

Age of Entry into work by the Illiterate Bhildren

Age of entry into work	Frequency	Percentage
6 to 7 Years	19	24.36
8 to 9 Years	11	16.37
10 to 11 Years	24	30.37
12 to 13 Years	6	7.69
15 to 18 Years	7	8.97
Not doing any work	9	11.54
Total	78	100.00

An attempt to know the age of entry into work by the illiterate children. (Table 6.7) indicates that about one fourth of them entered the work at the age of 6 to 7 years. 16.16 per cent at 8 to 9 years of age. Slightly less than one-third stated 10 to 11 years and a few others said 12 to 14 or 15 to 18 years of age as the age of entry into work. This analysis shows that in rural areas on overwhelming number of children have been entering the work force even before they attain the age of 10, which not only keep the children out of school, but also hinder their physical and psychological growth.

When enquired about the interest shown by teachers and village elite in enrolling the illiterate children in schools, an overwhelming majority of the parents said that nobody approached them in that regard.

The analysis shows that a large bulk of the illiterate children belong to poor families, poverty emerges as the main reason for child illiteracy. These children have been entering the work force at a tender age. The teachers and the village elite have been indifferent towards the education of poor children.

C. Parental Attitude Towards Stagnated Children

Stagnation is also considered as one of the important problems and it is more so in rural areas. The students studying in the same class for more than one year has several reasons. Here an attempt is made to examine the parental view-point towards the problem. Out of 205 respondents only 16 (7.81) belong to this category. The families are mainly poor or lower middle class.

The major reasons, as stated by the parents for stagnation, are; ill-health and lack of interest on the part of the teacher and the students.

With regard to their stage at which they got stagnated, out of 16 in three cases children got stagnated in class I, six in class II, two in class III, and three in class IV. Two in class V and X each. This analysis shows that the incidence of stagnation has been not very high. Whenever it is occurring, it is taking place at the primary level.

When asked about the parental efforts to make the children study properly, an overwhelming majority (68.75) said that they re-admitted their children in the school and others said that they arranged for private tuitions to see that they recover. A few admitted that they did not make any effort in this regard.

This analysis shows that stagnation is not very acute. The ill-health and indifference appear to be the main cause. The incidence of stagnation has been more at the primary stage. The parents continue to take some interest and not totally given up the education of the children.

D. Parent's Views on Functioning of the Village School

Parental attitude towards the village school and its functioning is crucial for development of rural education. Here are the view points of parents towards functioning of the village school.

To start with they were asked about nature of stay of the teachers. Nearly half of the parents said that the teachers are not staying in the village and reported that they are staying at the district headquarters and commute daily to the school. A few villagers said that the teachers reside in their respective native village and come to the school everyday. About 16 per cent of the parents did not know about the whereabouts of the teachers.

Further probing into the reasons for not staying in the villages reveals that the native places of the teachers were in close proximity. A considerable number of parents agreed that there are no housing facilities and drinking water has assumed alarming dimensions. A few parents also observed that due to availability of bus facilities teachers stay in the city where they can get better education to their children. A few villagers resented the urbanised attitudes of the teachers.

To a question with whom the teachers move closely in the village, about 40 per cent could not answer the question. From the rest on overwhelming majority stated that there has been no interaction between the teachers and community. A few other opined that the teachers meet sarpanches, village officers or members of parents committee and other big farmers. Thus the teachers have been alienated from the villages, even if they interact with the elite groups.

To another question about the proper functioning of the schools, about 47 per cent answered in the affirmative and 30 per cent in the negative. About 23 per cent could not answer the question. The respondents did express the feeling that

TABLE 6.8

Particulars of Government Aid to School Going Children

Class	Not getting anything	Getting Scholar-ships	Hostel	Mid-day Meal	Free Clothes, Meals	All Aids Except Hostel	Free Books Note-Books & Bags	Scholar-ships, Clothes, Books	Total
Rich	7(70.00)	2(20.00)	—	1(10.00)	—	—	—	—	10
Middle	42(47.73)	5(5.68)	—	35(39.77)	4(4.55)	2(2.77)	—	—	88
Poor	36(33.64)	9(8.41)	1(0.93)	37(34.58)	2(1.87)	14(13.08)	3(2.80)	5(4.67)	107
Total	85(41.46)	16(7.80)	1(0.48)	73(35.61)	6(2.92)	16(7.80)	3(1.46)	5(2.44)	205

the teachers never come to the school on the scheduled time and leave the school early. They come by undependable RTC buses. They opined that teachers do not take interest in teaching as there is none to question. They complained that the headmaster was not strict in these matters. They further stated that the accommodation is poor and the school is closed whenever it rains. On the whole they felt that their children go everyday to the school and come back home but learn nothing.

When asked about books and other stationery the responses reveal that a considerable number of parents from middle and poor class were not able to provide sufficient books to their children.

When enquired about the government aid (see Table 6.8) to their school-going children, about 41 per cent parents reported that their children did not get any aid from government. 7.80 per cent parents reported that their children got scholarships. They belong mostly to middle and poorer classes. About 35 per cent parents of middle and poor classes stated that their children were availing the facility of mid-day meal, but not getting other types of assistance from the government. About 8 per cent of the parents of SC and ST communities belonging to the middle and poor categories stated that their children were getting every thing except hostel facility. The analysis shows that there has been no uniformity in governmental assistance. Different children used to get different types of benefits. However, there were children who come from lower caste poorer families and were left uncovered.

TABLE 6.9

Satisfaction of Parents about Government Aid

(Those whose children got aid other than mid-day meal)

Response	Frequency	Percentage
Satisfied	5	10.64
Not satisfied	36	76.60
Did not respond or Don't know	6	12.76
Total	47	100.00

When asked about quality and quantity of the aid given by the government (Table 6 9) an overwhelming number (76.59) of them were not satisfied. Only a few (10.63) parents expressed their satisfaction.

When asked about the reasons for their dissatisfaction, most of them reported that the scholarship amount has been very meagre and needs to be raised. Others said that the quality of the clothes, school bags and slates, etc., supplied by the government was not good. They also reported that the clothes supplied do not suit the size of their children. And quality of those clothes has been very poor. They suggested that instead of giving clothes, it is better to give money which can be used for clothing purpose of their children. The slates and slate pencils also received similar type of comments. The general trend indicates the widespread resentment with the aid being given to the children.

The analysis of parental views on functioning of village school reveals that a majority of them felt that the teachers do not stay in the village and are not prompt in attending the school. The parents doubt the commitment of the teachers to their job. With regard to the interaction the data indicates that it is confined to the teachers and elite. They also expressed their unhappiness with the school accommodation and the assistance extended to the children by way of scholarships, clothes, slates, etc.

E. Parental Viewpoint on School-Society Relations

Here an attempt is made to examine the relations between the school and society. In the first place the parents were asked about the usefulness of the school to the villagers. To this question almost all the respondents answered in the affirmative. Most of them felt that the school can impart enlightenment and wisdom to the children and provide an opportunity for the children to get the education. They added that children have to trek long distances if there is no school in the village. A few parents felt that a school in the village not only enables the children to study but help parents in agricultural operations.

When enquired about the help that teachers can render for development of the village, half (49.75) of the respondents stated that teachers can do nothing for development of the village. They added that the teachers have grown quite selfish. About 23.41 per cent of the respondents said that the teachers can help for development. They cited the instance where the teachers evinced interest in constructing a new school building and collected donations for this purpose. However, 26.8 per cent of the respondents could not respond to this question.

To another question about teacher-parent interaction, nearly 90 per cent answered in the negative. They said that teachers meet the villagers only at the time of the census and enrolment of voters. The remaining 10 per cent said that the teachers meet them occasionally. The purpose of the visit in most of the cases is related to their personal matters. Sometimes the matters relating to the school also figure in. This shows the absence of interaction between the parents and the teachers.

To another question about the visits that the parents make to the teachers, more than half of them stated that they do not go to the teachers. About 40 per cent said that they go to the teachers occasionally to know about the progress of their children and to enquire about the scholarship amounts and other benefits. They also meet them on occasions like Republic Day or Independence Day.

When enquired about the efforts made by the villagers to develop the school, about 45 per cent respondents said that villagers made some efforts to develop the school by giving donations for expansion of the school building. Others stated that villagers took no interest in development of the school.

To another question, whether the parent himself has made any effort to develop the school, (Table 6.10) only 27.32 per cent of the parents, mostly from better off FC and BC sections made some effort to develop the school. They reported that they strived for upgradation of school and collected donations for the construction of school building. The remaining 72.68 per cent admitted that they made no effort to develop the school. They were mostly from middle and poorer class. Most of them said that nobody approached them for any help.

TABLE 6.10
Parental Efforts to Develop the School

Class	Caste	Made some effort	Did not make any effort	Total
Rich	FC	2(25.00)	6(75.00)	8
	BC	—	2(100.00)	2
	SC	—	—	—
	ST	—	—	—
Middle	FC	12(46.15)	14(53.85)	[illegible]
	BC	22(38.60)	35(61.40)	[illegible]
	SC	—	5(100.00)	[illegible]
	ST	—	—	—
Poor	FC	—	7(100.00)	7
	BC	17(24.29)	53(75.71)	70
	SC	2(7.69)	24(92.31)	26
	ST	1(25.00)	3(75.00)	4
Total		56(27.32)	149(72.68)	205

Some of them observed that they would not be able to help as they themselves were in difficulties.

This analysis of school-society relations reveals that, parents perceive school as a useful instrument for childrens education. Majority of them think that the teachers have not worked for development of the village. The interaction between the school and the villagers is almost absent.

F. Parental Opinion on Relevance of Education

The last dimension that is examined is the parents assessment about the relevance of present education.

In the first place they were asked to give their opinion on relevance of present education to the future life of the children. About 9 per cent said that it was not useful. More than half (58.05) of the parents said that the present education can be useful in getting some employment. About 22 per cent said that the present education is useful for the children to improve their knowledge and awareness. While a few felt it is useful to eke out livelihood, a few others said that it can be useful to go in for higher education. However, about 6 per cent could not answer. Those who said that the present education was not useful opted for technical education. And those who said it was useful felt that the educated people can get employed as teachers, lecturers, tahsildars, doctors, police officers, clerks and peons, etc. This shows that most of the parents who were sending their children to the school were hopeful that they get some employment in the organised sector (see Table 6.11).

When enquired about the necessity of vocational education in schools, except a few all the parents were in favour of introducing vocational education in schools. About the stage at which vocational education should be introduced, most of them opted for either at middle (6th to 7th class) or high school (8th to 10th class) level. A very few suggested primary level.

Further enquiry into the type of vocation that can be introduced in the schools, while 25 per cent could not answer, most of the respondents opted for tailoring, embroidery and

TABLE 6.11

Opinion of Parents on Relevance of Present Education

Opinion	Frequency	Percentage
Useful in getting some employment	119	58.05
Improve knowledge and awareness	45	21.95
Useful to eke out livelihood	7	3.42
Useful to go in for higher education	3	1.46
Not useful	19	9.27
Do not know	12	5.85
Total	205	100.00

trades like motor mechanism, welding, carpentry, etc. Others opted for certain skils such as training in agriculture, traditional caste occupations, poultry, driving, typewriting, etc.

When enquired about the suitability of school timings an overwhelming majority (92.21) are satisfied with the existing time. The others suggested changes as; 8 a.m. to 2 p.m., 9 a.m. to 4 p.m. Those who opted for existing timings (10 a.m. to 4 p.m) justified it on the grounds that most of the students have to come from other villages and it becomes difficult to such students to reach in time if it is changed. The general feeling about the timings and the need for a change in educational set-up do not appear to be enjoying the support of the rural people.

TABLE 6.12

Willingness of Parents to Allow their Children to do Physical Labour

Response	Frequency	Percentage
Not willing	168	81.95
Willing	37	18.05
Total	205	100.00

To know their values on physical labour (Table 6.12), a question was posed to them about their willingness to allow their children to do physical labour. An overwhelming majority (81.95) of parents belonging to all castes and all classes vehemently rejected the idea of their children doing physical labour. Most of the parents think that they themselves have been srugglingfor survival by doing manual labour and that type of 'fate' should not repeat in the case of their children. However, 18 per cent expressed their willingness to allow their children to do manual labour. Their logic is based on understanding that it is not possible for everybody to get a job. The pattern of reponses conclusively indicates the enormous damage that formal education has done to the work ethic.

To a subsequent question, more than 90 per cent felt that education saves the children from doing manual labour. The remaining parents said, that education may not save them from doing manual labour but it offers alternative sources of livelihood.

TABLE 6.13

Parental Opinion on Physical Labour

Response	Frequency	Percentage
Physical labour is more difficult	159	77.56
Mental labour is more difficult	34	16.58
Both are difficult	12	5.86
Total	205	100.00

When asked about the differences between physical labour and mental labour (Table 6.13), about 77 per cent thought physical labour was more difficult than mental labour. About 17 per cent thought the other way round. The preference for mental labour is also based on the ground that it is secure and comfortable. This is further confirmed when the respondents stated that they would not like their children to go for mental labour even in the event of physical labour being made more remunerative and attractive than the mental labour. For an overwhelming majority (83.41) felt that mental labour is more comfortable and involves less strain.

About introduction of compulsory education, more than 90 per cent approved the idea. They thought that it would lead to greater spread of education among the rural poor. When asked about the necessity of education to Harijans, Girijans and poor children, almost all the respondents opined that they must receive education. When asked to comment on girls education almost all of them unanimously approved girls education. However, they have some doubts, and reservations about its usefulness and impact.

When asked about their plans for future education of the children, a majority of them propose to educate them upto class X in view of their economic constraints. A few of them plan to send them for Inter or Graduation or any professional course like medicine and engineering.

When parents were asked to give their opinion on present education system (Table 6.14), a majority (68.78) of them could not answer. About 22 per cent reacted favourably about the present system. The rest of the respondents, a small number found fault with the system. Most of their complaints relate to the school administration, syllabus and punctuality of the teachers.

TABLE 6.14

Opinion of Parents on Present Education System

Opinion	Frequency	Percentage
Could not respond	141	68.78
It is alright	45	21.95
It is not functioning well	19	9.27
Total	205	100.00

The parents were asked to suggest improvements in the present education system. To this question three fourths of the respondents could not respond. The rest of them offered suggestions which are as follows ; teachers should behave in a responsible manner with regard to the rural education ; school buildings must be constructed in all villages so that there can be no interruption in education ; strength of teachers in each school should be raised so that effective teaching can be arranged ; technical education must be introduced, teachers should stay in the village where they are working so that they can avoid the delay in arriving to the schools ; the teachers from the same village should not be posted to the school ; hostel facilities should be provided in the villages, increase in number of schools and classes and strengthening vigilance over the teachers.

II. Attitudes of Village Elite Towards Rural Education

Next to the parents, the village elite constitute an important segment in rural sector. The development of village schools depends upon the interest and initiative of the village elite. For this purpose the sample of 50 village elite were drawn. Their socio-economic characteristics are as follows ;

TABLE 6.15

Caste Background of Village Elite

Caste	Frequency	Percentage
F.C.	20	40.00
B.C.	23	46.00
S.C.	7	14.00
Total	50	100.00

TABLE 6.16

Occupation of Village Elite

Occupation	Frequency	Percentage
Agriculture	35	70.00
Business	3	6.00
Tailoring	2	4.00
Toddy tapping	2	4.00
Labourer	2	4.0
Sheep and cattle rearing	2	4.00
Weaving	2	4.00
Others	2	4.00
Total	50	100.00

TABLE 6.17

Educational Levels of Village Elite

Education	Frequency	Percentage
Illiterate	12	24.00
Primary	19	38.00
Secondary	13	26.00
Intermediate	2	4.00
Graduation	4	8.00
Total	50	100.00

The Tables 6.15, 6.16 and 6.17 reveal that most of the elite come from Forward Castes and Backward Castes. A very few come from the Scheduled Castes. Most of them come from farming communities and a few come from the caste occupations. Most of them were either illiterates or studied upto primary or middle school levels. Position wise most of them were Gram Panchayat members and caste elders. A few of them were also village officials like police patels and patwaris.

A. Elite Opinion on School and its Functioning

To the enquiry about the infrastructural adequacy in terms of number of teachers, accommodation, black-boards, benches, play ground, games material, drinking water facility, library and toilet facilities, 75 per cent to 85 per cent of the elite unanimously expressed the opinion that nothing is sufficient and satisfactory in the schools.

With regard to the stay of the teachers in the village, most of them, according to the elite, were not staying in the village. The causes for this trend according to them are; the native places of the teachers were in close proximity with transport facilities, lack of facilities like drinking water in the villages; the teachers were accustomed to urban life and its facilities and proper housing facilities do not exist in the village.

About the consequence of teachers not staying at their work places, 28 per cent of the elite opined that it is of no consequence provided the teachers come to school in time. Others maintain that staying outside results in irregular attendance to the school. About the working of the teachers, the opinion of the elite is equally divided. While one section of the elite did not find any fault, another section held that the teachers have grown selfish and indifferent to their duties.

To another question about the distribution of books a large majoriry (62.00) of the village elite stated that they never reach the school in time. With regard to the government aid to the school children, three-fourths of the elite stated that the children belonging to BC, SC and ST communities were getting aid from the government. About the sufficiency of the amount, a considerable number of them did not know the details. However, more than half of the elite felt that the amount was not sufficient. About the school dress, slates, bags, books and other benefits, many of the elite have no knowledge. Those who have the knowledge expressed their dissatisfaction with the quality and quantity of these benefits.

B. Opinion on School-Society Relations

The elite were asked about the usefulness of a school to assess their perception of educational goals. To this question 40 per cent felt that having a school in the village results in awakening of the children and the people of the village. 20 per cent said that people would acquire the capacity to read and write; they can read letters, name plates and sign boards on buses and so on. About 10 per cent of the elite maintained that a school in the village would certainly shape the children into doctors, engineers and other employees. Another 18 per cent of the elite opined that it would ease the burden of the parents from sending their children to other village. The children would also be available to parents for other household and agricultural operations. (see Table 6.18).

About the nature of help that the teachers render to the development of the village, an overwhelming majority of the elite stated that teachers did nothing for development of the village. Some of them observed "we are happy that the teachers have not spoiled the village". However, about 28 per cent of the elite felt that the teachers helped the village in construction of school building and upgradation of the school.

TABLE 6.18

Elite Perception of Usefulness of School

Response	Frequency	Percentage
It awakens children and people	20	40.00
People acquire capacity of reading and writing	10	20.00
It would ease the burden of parents from sending children to other villages	9	18.00
It provides employment such as Doctors, Engineers, etc.	5	10.00
It helps poor to educate their children	4	8 .00
Children would be available to help parents in agricultural works	2	4.00
Total	50	100.00

About elite-teacher interaction, about two-thirds of the elite reported that teachers never contact them. One third of the elite were in contact with the teachers. To the question about the purpose of this contact, the elite said that teachers meet them either on special occasions or to discuss problems pertaining to school children or school development and sometimes in connection with their transfers and personal problems. Those elite who stated that the teachers do not go to them opined that the teachers meet only those elite with whom they have some work.

About the elite contacting the teachers, two thirds of the elite answered in the affirmative. This interaction is on the special occasions or during the school committee meetings or due to the schemes like scholarships and mid-day meal programme. The rest of the elite do not meet them as they do not find any reason to meet them.

When enquired about the villagers' help to the development of the school, most of the elite said that the villagers extended their help by donating money for the construction of school building. A few of the elite stated that the villagers were indifferent. They also felt that sometimes their interference was of negative type.

It is attempted to examine whether the elite help the school. More than half of the elite reported that they helped the school while 46 per cent did not take any interest.

C. Village Elite Attitude on Drop-out Problem

Regarding drop-outs in the school, 72 per cent of the elite agreed that there has been the problem of drop-outs. About the reasons for drop-outs, 36 per cent stated the main reason for drop-out has been wide spread poverty. About 14 per cent said agricultural work, 8 per cent said household work another 8 per eent traced it to daily wage labour. The other reasons include ill-health, early marriage, lack of proper facilities in the school, and failures in examinations (see Table 6.19).

With regard to the improvements to solve the problems of drop-outs, the suggestions include greater interest on the part of the parents, better facilities for poor children, personal attention to each child, compulsory education and over all improvement in economic conditions. When asked about their own role in improving the situation, most of them admitted that they did nothing in this regard.

TABLE 6.19

Elite Perception of Reasons for Drop-out

Reasons for Drop-out	Frequency	Percentage
Poverty and economic difficulty	18	36.00
Agricultural works	7	14.00
House-hold work	4	8.00
Going for daily labour	4	8.00
Lack of proper school facilities	4	8 00
Others	7	14.00
Don't know	6	12.00
Total	50	100.00

When the opinion of elite is sought on the existing non-detention system in schools, majority (74.00) of them opined that detention system should be restored. When asked for the reasons they said that detention would improve the standards of education. There is also small section which supported non-detention system on the ground that children would improve in the course of time.

D. Views of the Elite on Relevance of Present Education

Here an attempt is made to examine the opinion of rural elite on relevance of present education. 20 per cent of the elite said that the present education was not useful for future lives of the children and suggested vocational, scientific and technical education to be introduced in the place of the present education. About 30 per cent of the elite felt that the present education provides knowledge and awareness to the children. A large number of them opined that this education can provide employment for posts such as teacher, police officer, compounder, etc. The remaining elite stated that it helps the students for higher learning and to engage themselves in business and other activities for livelihood.

To a subsequent question about the need for introduction of vocational education in the schools, about 86 per cent favoured the introduction of vocational education. Those who favoured vocational education wanted either training in traditional caste occupations or in a particular trade or training in tailoring. They wanted vocational education to be introduced at upper primary or secondary level of school education.

About the suitability of existing school time (i.e., 10.00 a.m. to 4.00 pm) except a few who opted for 8.00 a.m. to 1.00 p.m. all the village elite approved the existing timings. Regarding the holidays and vacation to the school also, most of the elite did not find anything wrong with the present system of vacation. They maintained that all the seasons are less suitable for vacation.

With regard to the present education system and its working, 24 per cent could not answer. About 42 per cent did not find anything wrong with it. The rest of them felt that it is defective and not relevant. To the question for improvement of the present education system, a majority of the elite (56.00) could not offer any solutions. About 10 per cent of the elite suggested introduction of technical education. The other suggestions include introduction of detention system, insistence on teachers stay in the village, efforts to improve the standards of present education, greater commitment of the teachers and accessibility to education for all.

Values of elite are important. in understanding their role. The responses, broadly indicate the democratic attitudes on the part of the elite. Most of the elite supported cómpulsory education, better facilities for poor, encouragement for girls education. They pleaded that benefits should be extended on the basis of economic conditions and not on caste basis.

Summing-Up

The attitudes and perceptions of the parents reveal that most of them were sending their children with a hope that they would get jobs in the organised sector. They were found favouring vocational education such as tailoring, motor mechanic, poultry, welding, etc., at schools level itself. They were against their children doing manual labour even in the event of it fetching more income than mental labour. They felt that mental labour is more secure and comfortable. This type of change in the value system is the counter productive effect of education on work ethic.

An analysis of attitudes of parents towards rural education reveals that smaller the village the more the percentage of parents who send their children to other villages for education. The small village were devoid of educational facilities. Most of the poor parents have not been able to send the children to the school and have been facing economic difficulties. This is also true of certain lower middle class parents who were found dropping their children from studies because of economic difficulties and demands of agricultural and their other caste occupations. Most of the illiterate children come from poor families who cannot afford to send the children to school. On the contrary the children are pressed into service to eke their livelihood. The ill health and lack of interest on the part of the children account for stagnation. Most of the parents were neither satisfied with the way the schools have been functioning nor with the quality and quantum of assistance by the government. Yet all of them were favourable for spreading of education. Intimate school-community relations were absent. There was hardly any interaction between the teachers and the villagers. This indicates the weak community base of educational system.

The attitudes of village elite towards rural education were almost identical with that of the parents. They were also dissatisfied with the existing facilities and the teachers. The school-society relations have not been conducive for effective functioning. For the problems of inadequate coverage, dropouts and stagnation, they traced the cause to poverty. They also offered the same suggestions that parents offered. The pattern of responses broadly indicate, that elite do not evince much interest in matters of rural education, although they were favourably disposed towards spreading and democratising the education.

The perception and attitudes of the parents and elite broadly indicate that the existing facilities have been quite inadequate. The education is introducing a new work ethic opposed to the dignity of labour. As far as spreading of education is concerned, the pattern of response indicates that the social and economic conditions have not been conducive for universalisation of education. No extra effort is being made by any section of the society to achieve this goal. Given the present educational set up and its linkages with the socio-economic system, the goal of universalisation of education appears to be a remote possibility.

REFERENCES

1. Children who were at the time of this study, dropped from going to school, but had the school going age (i.e., 5 to 18) were considered. Childern who dropped from school but crossed 18 years were not considered for the study.
2. Here also illiterate children means, children of school-going age (5 to 18), but never attended the school. The illiterate children who crossed 18 years of age were not included in this category. Hence it is more number of families with all children being schooled.

7

Mid-Day Meals Programme

This chapter seeks to analyse the opinion of the parents, village elite and teachers on the mid-day meal programme. Since their opinions constitute a support base for any educational programme, their impressions on mid-day meal scheme are sought. The main purpose of the chapter is to examine the impact and the process involved in the scheme in attaining the goals of education, particularly universalisation.

The mid-day meal scheme is not totally new to either to India or to the state of Andhra Pradesh. On the recommendation of National School Health Committee, the Government of India initially introduced the mid-day meals scheme as centrally sponsored programme in 1962-63 in selected areas. Its objective was to provide supplementary nutrition of 300 calories with 8-12 grams of protein to children in the age group of 6-11 years.[1] There has been a programme of mid-day meal in Andhra Pradesh in 1960s[2] with the assistance of an American Organisation CARE (Co-operative for American Relief Everywhere). Under this scheme *uppuma* (made with corn flour) and milk were served to the children for which, corn flour, milk powder and edible oils were supplied by the CARE.

This programme has failed because of several problem. The headmasters of the schools were made solely responsible for implementation of the programme. They had to personally collect the material consisting of corn flour and milk powder, from the samithi office. There was neither transportation facility to deliver the provisions at school nor was there any financial provision for this purpose. Further, the headmasters were to mobilise local resources to meet the expenditure for cooking and distributing the food to the children. As a result those who were interested in the scheme alone took pains to collect the material from samithi office and implement the programme. Most of the teachers had no interest and the scheme remained unimplemented. There was also scope for misuse of the materials; the corn flour and milk powder in certain cases were misused and sold in the black market. Further the students were to bring with them their own plates and tumblers to have the food. Teachers had to take separate attendance every day of the students who participated in it. The CARE programme has been in implementation on paper and on a nominal basis.

The present mid-day meal programme existed at the time of the study has been in implementation in the villages under study along with the state wide programme introduced from November 14, 1982. The mid-day meal scheme which formed part of the 1982 election manifesto of the Telugu Desam Party had been actually inaugurated by the then Congress (I) Chief Minister K. Vijaya Bhaskar Reddy, on November 14, 1982, just before the 1983 assembly poll to prove that it was a programme of the Congress Party.[3] The same programme was continued after the Telugu Desam Party came to power in 1983.

The scheme which was introduced keeping in mind the objective of universalisation of elementary education, is however, an admission of wide-spread poverty and its role in universalisation of education. The main objectives of the programme have been;[4] (i) increasing the enrolment of children in the age group of 6 to 11 years. (ii) prevention of drop-out rate of children in the classes one to five, (iii) ensuring regularity of attendance and (iv) providing nutritious food to the children in the school going age.

Under this scheme children were served with rice and sambar and sometimes with rice and vegetable curry. Each student is provided with a meal containing hundred grams of rice, five grams of Dal and three ounces of oil. Separate cooks have been appointed to prepare the meals. Each cook is paid Rs. 75 per month. Headmasters were incharge of preparing and distributing the food to the students. Subsequently, this responsibility has been transferred to village sarpanches.

This new programme also faced several problems, as they did not learn any lessons from the past experience. Several cases of misuse of the material have been reported. In addition, the following problems are reported. Schools have become kitchen centres. Teachers have become over burdened; they have stopped teaching as their time is spent in preparation and distribution of food. Teaching schedule has been upset. Schools were not provided with sufficient equipment and infrastructure for preparation of the meals. Stocks were not reaching the schools regularly and in time. Students and parents were found dissatisfied with the food because of its low quality and bad preparation. The programme ; almost came to a halt with the handing it over to the sarpanches.

Here an attempt is made to examine the perceptions of parents, teachers and village elite on the problems in implementation of the programme. The new mid-day meal programme has been implemented since its inception in the three selected villages. Earlier the CARE programme was implemented for some time in the two villages and in village 'Peta' it was not implemented. Regarding the new mid-day meal scheme, since the 'Peta' village has a single teacher school that too with an irregular teacher, the programme has not had much impact on the education in the village. On the contrary, it is believed that it had a negative effect on functioning of the school. For whatever little time the teacher had for teaching was diverted to the mid-day meal operations. Since he was the only teacher, he could not look after teaching and mid-day meal operations simultaneously. Several times, it is reported that the meals was not served to the pupils. Villagers complained that there were pilferages or the cooks were not honest and took away the food for his family members. Some of the other problems include; no provision for water to wash the hands and plates, food is served outside in the dust which gets mixed up with the food, the places of cooking and distribution were not hygenical.

The problems of mid-day meal in 'Konda' village were different from that of 'Peta' village. Since 'Konda' has an upper primary school, it had six teachers. All of them were found sharing the food meant for pupils. They also faced similar problems. However, the problems stemming from untouchability are unique to this village. In the initial stages, only backward class people were recruited as cooks and workers. The Harijans were deliberately excluded. The Harijans protested and got two of their members included as cooks. Although Harijans have joined as cooks, they were not allowed to prepare the food. They were entrusted with the task of collecting fire-wood, separating foreign material from the rice and fetching water from the well. There are cases where the Harijans have not been allowed to fetch even water from the well. Since the Harijans were associated with food operations, the forward caste parents withdrew their children from eating the mid-day meal at school. In addition to these problems, the low wages paid to the cooks and workers added to the gravity of the situation. They have been working for low wages with the hope that their services would be regularised.

The village 'Kur' faced another type of problems. It has a secondary school and an upper primary school. Since the programme was meant only to primary sections, it has not been extended to secondary school students. This led to different levels of involvement of the teachers. Since there was fourteen teachers, it was a divided house. This is bound to affect the mid-day meal scheme too. From the fourteen teachers a few teachers advised the headmaster to buy some equipment to the school by manipulating the provisions of mid-day meal. For this purpose they suspended serving the food to pupils on a few days on the plea that they were busy in conducting unit tests or having some meeting. They sold away the rice, dal and oil, thus saved, in the market. The amount was quite substantial as it was accumulated by not serving the meal to 600 students for about a week. With this amount they purchased a steel almirah and some utensils. They had a dinner party with sweets. As there were divisions among the teachers, this was leaked out to the public and a complaint was lodged with the Panchayat Samithi. On 20th February, 1982, the Assistant Collector made a preliminary enquiry into the matter and found that the mid-day meal programme has been mis-managed. The headmaster of the school was transferred and a thorough enquiry was ordered From the day (20th February 1982) onwards the programme was suspended for two months. In the meanwhile, the headmaster managed to get his transfer cancelled. Subsequently when the programme was trasferred to Sarpanches, the Sarpanch of 'Kur' village was reluctant to take up the programme for quite some time. This also resulted in suspension of the programme once again for another two months. Thus, the programme operated on a very irregular fashion. The villagers were also found dissatisfied with the way the whole programme has been managed. There was no caste problem as the Harijans were excluded very intelligently and they also did not protest as they did in the other village. The school watchman—a Muslim—was acceptable to all the castes. It was so planned that the watchman and his family members were recruited to manage the scheme and Harijans were totally avoided.

I. Parents' Views on Mid-day Meal Programme

To have an indepth understanding of the functioning of the programme an attempt is made to elicit the opinion of the parents on mid-day meal programme. In all 205 parents were interviewed with the help of a structured questionnaire. These are the parents who expressed their attitudes on various dimensions of educational administration in the earlier part of this study.

To a question about sending their children to the school on account of the mid-day meal programme—a new facility—only 4.39 per cent said that they sent their children because of the programme. Most of them come from the very poor Scheduled

Caste and Backward Caste families. Those who did not send the children because of the programme observed, 'we can feed our children from whatever we possess'. A few backward caste parents said, 'we are sending our children to private school. We continue to send to private school although mid-day meal is provided in the government (Panchayati Raj) school because the standards of education in government school are quite poor'. The parents from rich and middle classes felt that it is below their dignity to allow their children to eat food along with the children of poorer families. Some of them opined that it amounts to begging the food. This type of value system operates in the case of certain families on whom a scheme like mid-day meal cannot make much impact. Thus, the scheme could only attract a negligible number of students from poor families and thus of marginal value in the universalisation of education.

To another question about the response of parental group to mid-day meal programme, all the parents belonging to middle and poor families were positive about the programme and their children were participating in the mid-day meal (Table 7.1). From the rich class about 75 per cent of the children were advised by their parents not to participate in the scheme. These children participated in the programme for sometime. The children from forward castes and rich and upper middle class did not participate right from the beginning. This shows that mostly children from higher class-caste were not participating in the mid-day meal scheme while the lower class-caste people were availing the facility.

The parents who withdrew the children from the mid-day meals were asked the reasons. The response pattern is varied. The reasons include—(1) lack of cleanliness and unhygenic conditions at the place of cooking and serving the food resulting in bad health; (2) children found, dead insects and housefly in the food and stopped eating ; (3) the preparation of the food is not done properly ; (4) there is mixing of foreign material like broken rice, small stones, pieces of glass and iron etc. (5) the children are not liking the taste of food and it cannot be compared with home food. There are also some

TABLE 7.1

Particulars of Parents whose Children Stopped MID-Day Meal in the Middle

Class/Caste	Stopped	Did not	Never went to	No opportunity to attend it	Total
Rich					
FC	—	1(12.50)	3(38.50)	5(50.00)	8
BC	1(50.00)	—	—	1(50.00)	2
SC	—	—	—	—	—
ST	—	—	—	—	—
Middle					
FC	4(15.38)	4(15.28)	10(38.46)	8(30.77)	26
BC	10(17.54)	29(50.88)	2(3.50)	16(28.08)	57
SC	—	4(80.00)	—	1(10 50)	5
ST	—	--	—	—	—
Poor					
FC	3(42.86)	2(28.57)	—	2(28.57)	7
BC	12(17.14)	29(41.43)	6(8.57)	23(31.86)	70
SC	1(3.85)	23(88.46)	—	2(7.69)	26
ST	—	4(100.00)	—	—	4
Total	31(15.12)	96(46.83)	21(10.25)	57(27.80)	205

parents who reported that the children were feeling shy to eat in a large group. This indicates the operational problems in a sensitive scheme like mid-day meal.

An enquiry into the causes for not allowing the children to participate in the scheme right from the beginning, the parents said that they did not like the children to take their own plates and tumblers like beggers. The other causes include—uncleanliness, involvement of Harijans and washermen in cooking, eating with Harijan boys, and can feed the boys at home itself. Thus, class and caste consciousness was deeply rooted in these parents who were opposed to their children participating in the scheme.

An attempt is made to know their awareness about the type of food and its contents, about 40.5 per cent stated that mid-day meal contains rice and samber. About 25 per cent said rice, sambar and vegetable curry. This means 65 per cent have some knowledge about the programme. The rest of the parents were not aware of the scheme at all. The items they mentioned like oil-rice, eggs, etc., were not a part of the mid-day meal scheme at all.

When enquired into the sufficiency of the food (100 grams rice+5gram dal) 30 per cent parents felt that it was sufficient, 37 per cent reported that it was not sufficient. Thirty-three per cent did not answer as they did not know about the details of the scheme. Those parents who thought it was insufficient reported that children were asking for food immediately after coming from the school, the children complained that the food is served only once and not served second time even when requested.

When asked to suggest alternative contents for mid-day meals (Table 7.2), 11 per cent did not answer, 14 per cent supported continuance of the scheme. About 17 per cent pleaded for total winding up of the scheme. About the changes, 22 per cent pleaded that the curries must be changed every day instead of serving sambar monotonously.

About 12 per cent suggested bread and milk as mid-day meal. Another 12 per cent pleaded for an egg each day along with rice and sambar. The remaining parents suggested inclusion of mutton and eggs in the meal. Some suggested mutton at least once in a week. These responses indicate that the parents expect the quality of the food to be improved.

TABLE 7.2

Parents' Suggestions for Alternative Contents for Mid-day Meals

Suggestion	Frequency	Percentage
Curries must be changed every day	45	21.96
Wind-up the scheme	34	16.58
Continue the existing scheme	30	14.63
Bread and Milk	25	12.20
Include egg in the meals	24	11.70
Include eggs and mutton	11	5.38
Mutton atleast once in a week	10	4.87
Milk and biscuits	3	1.46
Did not answer	23	11.00
Total	205	100.22

When enquired about the management of the mid-day meal programme in their respective villages, about 39 per cent stated that they have no complaints and another 32 per cent reported that they were not aware of the way the scheme is being managed. 28 per cent of the parents complained that there were irregularities and the scheme was mis-managed.

The 28 per cent who reported mismanagement mentioned unhygienic conditions at the place of cooking and serving the food. The food was not served regularly and all the days. The teachers were eating the food meant for children. Teaching was disturbed because of the scheme. Following are some of the comments made by the parents regarding the functioning of mid-day meal scheme in their villages ; 'It is true that this programme is providing food to students and teachers, but the education of children is spoiled by this programme. The time of the teachers is being wasted in preparing and serving the food instead of educating the children'. 'It has benefited the teachers and peons', 'spoiled rice containing white insects was served in the food' ; 'they are mixing up Harijan boys with others causing inconvenience to the other caste boys', 'lot of dust is being thrown up while they are eating', 'water is not being served to children while they are eating', 'small stones, insects, glass pieces and iron pieces are found in the food', 'the children are suffering from itching and vomiting on account of edible oil used in preparation of the food'. 'the food has not been served on several occasions on the grounds that there is no stock'. These comments do indicate the nature of the problems encountered in the implementation of the scheme.

When asked to suggest improvements in the programme, the parents suggested ; fine rice and fine oil should be used and cleanliness be maintained ; serving bread and milk which involves less time and energy ; giving scholarships instead of food ; the amount spent on each child may be given to the child ; plates and tumbler should be available in the school itself ; the separation of mid-day meal scheme from the school administration. A few suggested winding up of the programme and diversion of those funds for development of the school infrastructure.

The class-caste analysis indicates that poor Harijans and backward caste people were in favour of retaining the programme intact or with some modifications like separating the programme from schools, giving bread and milk, changing the vegetables, etc. Most of the upper caste-class people were for abandoning the programme and diverting this amount to school construction or direct payment to the children or their families.

Some of the responses are reproduced here for a sharper focus. 'It is better to give amount to the children in the shape of scholarships on the basis of their attendance and see that the expenditure incurred in mid-day meals in distributed among the children to avoid all irregularities in the scheme.' 'Even changes like substituting bread have problems, there is a possibility of bread being spoiled in the storage'; 'this dirty meal scheme should be wound up' ; 'construct school buildings instead of wasting money on mid-day meal', 'because of mid-day meal programme, the afternoon session of the school is being wasted' ; 'this scheme is causing deterioration in eduation, it is better to appoint wardens and separate the programme from schools' ; 'preparation of meals involve wastage of time and effort, it is better to serve bread, fruits and milk', 'it is difficult for all the children to bring every day plates and tumblers from their houses' ; 'children would feel shy to carry plates with them' ; 'children should be provided with sufficient food and water to drink and wash the plates and hands'. The pattern of response, it is noticed, is largely shaped by the class and caste background.

II. Opinion of village Elite on Mid-day Meal Programme

Village elite play a crucial role in a scheme like mid-day meal. It becomes difficult to implement the programme without their support and cooperation. It is for this reason the opinions of the village elite are elicited to assess their interest and involvement.

TABLE 7.3

Elite Perception of Impact of Mid-day Meal Scheme in Increase of School Strength

Response	Frequency	Percentage
Strength increased	27	54.00
Did not increase	18	36.00
Could not answer	5	10.00
Total	50	100.00

The village elite were asked about the impact of the mid-day-meal scheme on the school strength (Table 7.3). About 54 per cent of the elite thought that there has been increase in the strength ranging between ten to 150. However, 36 per cent reported no impact and 10 per cent could not answer the question. To another question about the drop-outs from the mid-day meal scheme, a large number of them reported that there were hardly any cases of drop-outs.

Regarding the supply of provisions like rice, edible oil, pulses, and other necessaries like cooking vessels, considerable number of the elite are found satisfied. There were a few elite who opined that these materials were inadequate to meet the demand. An overwhelming majority of them knew the components of mid-day meal. This indicates how the elite have been keeping themselves informed about the scheme.

With regard to the sufficiency of the food given under the mid-day meal scheme a large number of them opined that it was not sufficient. They said that the children go home and demand the food again. One member of the elite reported that when he went to the school to watch the mid-day meal programme, he noticed that the rice was served without curry or sambar. On an enquiry he was told that the stocks of pulses and tamarind were exhausted. A few elite observed that the insufficiency is caused on account of teachers sharing the food. On the whole the elite convey an impression that the quantity was not sufficient.

About the caste feelings with regard to the appointment of cooks, a few elite reported that parents of forward castes are unhappy about the appointment of Harijans and other low people as cooks and workers in the programme. The upper caste parents started preventing their children from participating in the programme. This was the experience in one of the villages taken up for the study. In the other two villages there were no complaints as no Harijan was appointed either as cook or worker. In these villages the men from the intermediate castes, who are acceptable to all castes, have been appointed as cooks. That is how in some places they eliminated Harijans to aviod such problems.

About the overall performance of the mid-day meal programme in their villages, 46 per cent of the elite did not find any major defect with it. However, more than half of the elite were dissatisfied. The reasons for dissatisfaction are many and varied. They pointed out that there were a number of operational constraints in the scheme. This includes the following reasons ; firstly, the school education is adversely affected by the programme as the students always look to kitchen and the teachers have to exert a lot in the scheme ; secondly, there were difficulties in getting fire wood, cooking vessels, etc ; thirdly, the precious time of the teacher is consumed by this scheme ; fourthly, teachers were abusing the programme and were indulging in mal-practices and unhealthy methods ;

fifthly, food is not of good quality and the mix of foreign material like small stones and other items is high and there are also instances when some dead insects were noticed ; sixthly, the cooks and workers were paid low wages and they were not trained for the job ; and lastly the supply of stocks has been erratic and the supplies have not arrived in time. These responses indicate the cultural hang-overs on the one hand, and the ill-prepared and ill-equipped programme on the other.

When asked for their suggestions to improve the mid-day meal programme, the village elite suggested varied measures. About 20 per cent of the elite supported the continuance of the scheme. The rest of them made the following suggestions ; (i) the students should be provided with money in the form of scholarships, free books, clothes, etc., instead of wasting money on mid-day meals, (ii) once in a week the children should be given egg or mutton along with meals ; (iii) mid-day meals should be entrusted to a separate agency or hostel and be delinked with the schools. They further suggested that it can be entrusted to some voluntary organisation like Mahila Mandals in the villages or to hostels which have already been established, in the rural areas.

III Teachers' Views on Mid-day Meal Programme

In this part an attempt is made to examine the opinions of teachers regarding the mid-day meal programme. Teacher is a category which was initially directly involved in management of the programme. The scheme was transferred to the Sarpanches at a later stage. It is their involvement that renders their opinions quite important for the purpose of analysis.

In the first place, it is attempted to know whether the attendance improved because of the mid-day meal programme. Since the secondary school teachers were not concerned with the programme, they were not aware of the details and dynamics of the programme. The teachers of primary and upper primary school reported increase in attendance. About the percentage of increase in attendance there is a variation in their estimation. It varies between ten per cent to thirty per cent. However, most of the teachers informed that the attendance that they have in the forenoon was not seen in the afternoon. This obviously indicates that the increase in attendance due to the mid-day meal programme may not contribute to the improvement in the overall performance of the boys in education.

Majority of these teachers opined that there was also increase in the overall strength in the school due to mid-day meal scheme. Commenting on the increase of the strength some teachers opined that it was actually not an increase in the students but an increase in the boarders. There were instances where the boys who were participating in a mid-day meal scheme were not registered students. Their names could not be enrolled as the scheme was introduced in the middle of the academic year.

To another question whether any student had dropped out from the mid-day meal scheme, except a very few cases, the incidence of drop-outs is reported to be negligible. However, a few teachers said that the students mostly from Reddy community did not eat the meal right from the beginning. This was the case with students from a few other forward castes. The teachers reported that about 20 boys dropped out after about ten days because of the caste feeling. This confirms that a section of the upper strata continues to cling to the old value system—the strangle hold of which is not weakened.

To a question whether the amount provided for the maintenance of mid-day meal programme (for vessels, firewood, etc. i.e., 10 paise per student) was sufficient to meet the requirements of the programme, a majority of the teachers answered in the negative. Those teachers who felt it was not sufficient reported that sometimes the expenditure was met from headmaster's pocket or public contribution. (See Table 7.4)

About the sufficiency of the quantity of food served (Table 7.5) 35 per cent of the teachers had no knowledge of the scheme, 37 per cent of the teachers said that it was sufficient. The remaining 28 per cent felt that the quantity served was not sufficient. They further opined that it was sufficient to small kids, but not for grown-ups of class IV and class V. They suggested that the rural children should be served 200 grams of rice instead of present 100 grams.

TABLE 7.4

Teachers' Perception of Sufficiency of the Amount Provided for the maintenance of Mid-day Meal Scheme

Response	Frequency	Percentage
Sufficient	7	21.88
Not sufficient	13	40.62
Don't know	12	37.50
Total	32	100.00

TABLE 7.5

Teachers' Perception of Sufficiency of Quantity of Food Served to the Children

Response	Frequency	Percentage
Sufficient	12	37.50
Not Sufficient	9	28.13
Do not know	11	34.37
Total	32	100.00

When enquired about the students getting their own plates and tumblers every day, most of the teachers expressed that the practice should be given up and the government must make an alternative arrangement. They added that the students are already over-burdened with a head-load of books and adding additional burden is not advisable. It is also stated that some students were losing them in the school. Most of the students rush to their homes at meal time to get the plates and run back after the meal to leave the plates. It not only wastes his time but causes undue exertion to the child. Some students who go home to return the plates do not come back to school. They stay at home for the rest of the day. It is also noticed that some students were concentrating more on getting plates than on getting the books to the school. About 19 per cent of the teachers opined that it is better that the students get their own plates and tumblers both, from the health point of view and enormous expenditure involved for the government in buying them.

Answering another question except a very few teachers all others reported that introduction of mid-day meal scheme added additional burden to the teaching community. The additional burden is caused, according to the teachers, on account of preparation and distribution of food to children. The whole process is complicated and the part of distribution is found to be extremely time consuming. The following are some of the comments of teachers about the burden because of mid-day meal; 'We have to spend most of our time in getting the meal prepared'.' It needs continuous guidance as the cooks and workers have no experience'. 'It is becoming inevitable for all the teachers to part take not only in preparing and serving food, but protecting and maintaining the record about the mid-day meal material'. 'We are getting delayed for our lunch every day'. 'We are getting tired after serving food and water to 600 students who sit in several rows'. 'Our difficulties in dealing with mid-day meals can be realised only when one witnesses it, it cannot be described'. 'The mid-day meal scheme reduced us into cooks and servers'. 'Until now teachers have been trained only in teaching, but from now onwards they have to be trained in cooking also'. These comments do indicate the nature of difficulties and the problems inherent in managing a scheme which calls for different attitudes and skills for which the teachers are least prepared.

An investigation into the overall impression of the teachers on mid-day meal scheme reveals that only one fifth of the teachers were positive about it and gave positive answer saying that there is nothing seriously wrong with the scheme. The rest of them felt that education suffered a great deal on account of this scheme. They also maintained that the management of the scheme ran into a number of problems, as it has not been well thought over and properly planned. As a result a large number of the teachers suggested winding up of the scheme and introduce benefits like scholarships.

Finally the interest of the government in the programme also declined because of financial difficulties. The Telugu Desam government which allocated Rs. 50 crores for the programme in its budget for 1983-84 ; allocated only Rs. 33 crores in its budget for 1984-85. The state's budget for 1985-86 made no mention of the scheme. Ultimately the government dropped the programme in 1985 on the grounds of corruption and unsatisfactory implementation.

Summing-up

The mid-day meal scheme was an important measure to achieve the twin objectives of educational policy, viz., universal enrolment and prevention of drop-outs. The scheme was introduced in the later part of 1982. The scheme as such is neither new to the state of Andhra Pradesh nor to the villages taken up for this study. Such a scheme was in vogue in the early sixties. It was financed and supported under American CARE programme. The scheme had to be wound up as it ran into a number of operational difficulties. The new mid-day meal scheme could have been caste in the light of earlier experience. But the study indicates that the scheme was facing similar problems that the CARE scheme faced in sixties. Finally the scheme met with the same fate that the earlier scheme met with.

An examination of the operation of the scheme in the three villages revealed that in the single teacher school, it was not only that the scheme had no positive impact but the teachers who used to spend some time in teaching became busy with the management of mid-day meal. The villagers complained of pilferages both by the cook and the teacher. The scheme did not take care of even the minimum requirements like water for drinking purposes, a protected shelter for eating the food, maintaining hygienical conditions both at the cooking and eating places. In the upper primary school, while the problems were identical, they had some different dimensions. The one problem they faced was the problem of untouchability. While Harijans insisted on being included in the whole mid-day meal operations, the upper castes resisted it. When the Harijans were appointed, the upper castes did not allow their children to part-take in the meal. In the third village while they eliminated Harijans very intelligently. They faced a different type of crisis. Since the upper primary school is a part of secondary school, there were fourteen teachers. It is the 'politics' of the teachers that affected the scheme adversely. The relations among the teachers got strained in the process of manipulating the mid-day meal scheme. The scheme got suspended for some time because of the factions and differences among the teachers. Thus, the experience in all the three villages sharply reveals the inadequacies in terms of manpower and infrastructure, stranglehold of traditional value set up and the divisions and factions among the teachers and their manipulations. All these factors severely affected a well intentioned mid-day meal scheme.

A further investigation has been made into the attitudes and perceptions of the parents, elite and teachers to gain a deeper insight into the dynamics of an important measure intended for universalisation of education. The responses of parents indicate that only about less than five per cent of the parents sent their children to the school because of the scheme. The attitudes towards mid-day meal programme were sharply divided. While the parents from lower middle and poorer classes were positive towards the scheme, the parents from upper middle and rich were negatively disposed towards the scheme. For the parents from the upper strata had a number of complaints against the bad management of the programme. They also maintained that children were being treated as beggars under the scheme. The parents belonging to the poorer sections, while reacted positively towards the scheme as such, were critical about its implementation. They said that the food was monotonous, stale, insufficient and adulterated. They also reported mis-management of the scheme by the teachers. They sought for improvement in the quality and quantity of the meal, better infrastructure, separation of meals management from the school management. The parents from the upper castes and classes pleaded for winding up of the scheme and diversion of funds for building construction and further strengthening of the infrastructure.

An analysis of the elite responses also revealed similar trends that are seen in the case of parents. The elite agreed that the strength of students in the school increased. But they felt that the provisions given for the meal were inadequate. They admitted that caste feelings were operating very actively They highlighted a number of operational difficulties in the management of the scheme. In their overall response while a section of the elite pleaded for continuance and improvement in the scheme, another section advocated for abandonment of the scheme. The sharp divisions in the opinions and attitudes were rooted in their socio-economic status in the rural society.

The teachers—another vital components of rural education-took a more bitter and negative attitudes towards the scheme. The teachers like the elite agreed that mid-day meal has a positive impact on the attendance and over-all improvement in the student strength in the school. However, they observed that the boys were found more interested in the scheme than in education. The teachers also felt that the infrastructure to manage the scheme was inadequate and the quantities supplied insufficient. They personally thought that the scheme adversely affected the teaching community and added a lot of physical burden to their work, and new tensions in work place. A large number of teachers pleaded for abandonment of the scheme, on the ground that it has not been well thought over and properly planned.

An analysis of a well intentioned public measure to universalise education, indicate how inadequate planning and hasty implementation can defeat the purpose for which it is initiated. The conception of the scheme is defective as it has not taken several factors into account, inspite of earlier experience with a similar scheme. The implementation floundered because of inadequate infrastructure and weak support from the upper strata. This is one example where one can notice the cobwebs of rural cultural set-up, and their adverse impact on a policy. Absence of a built-in counter-strategy indicates the shallowness of a programme like mid-day meal for poor rural children. The ultimate abandonment of the scheme which was meant for rural poor indicates the nature of political will and its commitment to universalisation of education.

REFERENCES

1. Ghanshyam Shah, *Evaluation of Mid-day Meals Scheme : An Interim Report* (Cycle), Centre for Social Studies, Surat, 1987, p. 2
2. G.O. Ms. No. 3112/D/2/November 23, 1984 was issued to this effect.
3. M. Shatrugna, No Mid-day Meals for poor children, *Economic and Political Weekly*, Vol. xx, No. 21, May 25, 1985, p. 898
4. S. Rami Reddy, *Study of Implementation of Mid-day Meal Programme Summary* (Cycle), Centre for Planning and Development Studies. Andhra University, Waltair, 1985, p.3
5. M. Shatrugna, *op cit.*

8

Summing-Up

Education is a crucial variable in any development strategy. The relation between education and development can be seen all over the world; the countries which are more developed are those which have higher level of literacy. Education has all the potential to bring about changes in the social, political, economic and cultural aspects of human life. It can not only help in higher skill formation for the release of productive forces but concientize the people and cause qualitative change in human relations. In an ancient society like India, education was meant for a small privileged section and others were denied access to it. The secularisation of educational opportunities was initiated during the British period and the objective of universalisation of education has been accepted as a national goal after Independence. Although, it was envisaged in the Indian Constitution that this goal would be realised in a decade, the experience indicates that it is not only that the nation is far off from the goal but the number of illiterates, in absolute numbers, increased during the last four decades. The incidence of illiteracy is far higher in the rural areas. It is this phenomenon that needs to be investigated and explained.

During the post-Independence period, committees and commissions examined the problem and made innumerable recommendations. A few researchers who probed into the problem highlighted the constraints in education. However, educational administration continues to be a neglected area. The present study sought to investigate into the policy and administrative dimensions of education in rural areas. This study is based on empirical data and mainly analyses the causes for the gap between promise and performance in universalisation on education. It examined four schools located in three villages in a Telangana district of Andhra Pradesh. For the purpose of this study the sample is drawn from the parents, elite, students and teachers. The problems and perceptions of these sections were presented. The main areas that study covered are; the conduciveness of the socio-economic environment, the suitability of organisational set-up, the problems and perceptions of students and teachers, the attitudinal pattern of elite and parents and the impact of mid-day meal scheme.

An analysis of the environment of education in the district as well as in villages selected for the study showed that the socio—economic environment in rural areas was not conducive for expansion and advancement of education. Though the district has had educational schemes right from the pre-independence days at aggregate level, it lags behind in educational development compared to the other regions and whole state. Since the economic means and political institutions have been in the hands of the upper strata, a majority of the Scheduled Castes and backward class people have been looked up in the basic struggle for survival. They neither have the access, nor can avail the facilities offered in the present system.

The rural education is further handicapped as the existing rural educational institutions suffer from lack of proper accommodation and inadequate physical equipment and learning material. A majority of the teachers do not stay in the villages where they are working. The village elite and better off sections have not been evincing much interest in improving educational institutions in the villages. Most of them sent their children to the town or city schools. The inefficiency and unpopularity of the government schools is giving rise to private schools even in the rural areas. The poor children cannot attend these schools as they are expensive and do not offer any concessions.

The government continues to be indifferent towards the management of rural educational institutions. The people, who are engaged in the basic struggle for livelihood neither have interest nor the time to build pressure from below for improving the quality and quantity of educational institutions. The study indicates that only fifty per cent of the children of school going age were in the schools and the rest of them were outside the school system. This itself is an evidence indicating the remoteness of the educational system from its goals. The overall social and economic environment in rural areas has not been conducive for development of the education and its institutions to achieve the constitutional goal of universalisation of elementary education.

An analysis of organisational and institutional set up for education in rural areas showed that the existing set up is continuation of the system that was developed during the British colonial rule and feudal princely state. Though some changes were effected in the administrative set-up, they did not touch the basic structure. For instance till 1965 there were administrative units at state, regional and field levels. The set-up at the regional level was scrapped in 1965 and the district level was sought to be strengthened by elevating the position of District Educational Officer to the status of a Deputy Director. However, the regional set-up with Regional Joint Directors has been revived in the year 1982. The changes that were introduced at the state level revolved around bifurcation, unification and rebifurcation of Directorate of Public In struction.

At the grass-roots level no significant changes have been effected. The introduction of Panchayati Raj system and placing a large number of schools under it was considered a significant development in the evolution of grass-roots educational administration. It was hoped that the political leadership would evince greater interest in the problems of rural education.

This system failed to accomplish the objectives of universalisation of education on the one hand and to effect substantial democratic decentralisation of administration on the other. The discussions with officials of Panchayati Raj schools revealed that the government retained its right of control over Panchayati Raj schools on the plea that the finances flow from the state exchequer. In academic matters the grip is tightened in the name of technical control. This takes away the initiative from Panchayati Raj bodies and inhibit the independent development of these institutions.

Administratively the rural schools are under Panchayati Raj institutions and technically under State Education Department. While the salaries of the teachers are paid by the government, the Panchayati Raj bodies exercise day-to-day administrative control. Due to dual management, neither the government has full control nor the Panchayati Raj. For instance, the Panchayati Raj teachers do not take the state inspecting authority seriously as the disciplinary action is to be initiated by Panchayati Raj bodies. Thus, the administration suffers in terms of its control and direction.

While the administrative set-up is having several deficiencies, the physical equipment of the schools has not been adequate for promotion of healthy education in rural areas. An analysis of the physical conditions of the schools revealed that they suffer from lack of accommodation, furniture, sanitation facilities, library books, science equipment, inadequate and poor quality of financial aid and assistance from the government. The study also indicates that smaller the school, the more it suffers.

The defective administrative machinery, weak grass-roots management and poor physical conditions reduce the quality and quantity of education in rural areas. Such school management cannot attain either universalisation of education, nor can it create skilled manpower in the rural sector. Consequently, neither it can help for higher production nor for a change in the overall human relations.

The third dimension that is examined is the problem and perceptions of the teachers, parents, elite and students. The teachers constitute an important dimension in the educational administration. An analysis of social background of the teachers indicates that most of them come from backward castes with reasonable academic qualifications and trained skills. While their origins were in rural areas, they received their education in urban areas. They categorised themselves largely as middle class. The middle class nature of the teachers largely shapes their perceptions.

The perceptions of the teachers with regard to the infrastructure confirms the earlier finding that the infrastructure has been quite inadequate. Some of the schools do not have even full complement of the teachers. They resented the existing conditions and facilities and considered that it was not conducive for sound education. Even in those cases where the facilities were extended, they thought it is neither given in sufficient quantity nor in time.

Regarding the teacher-community relations, there has been a general feeling of alienation on the part of the teachers from students and village people. In the case of students, the teachers have come to feel not only that they do not enjoy respect of the students but have to face their growing indiscipline. In the case of villagers, the interaction between the school and village is largely absent. They also felt that the rural elite have no respect for the teachers. The parental Committees, which are intended to provide a forum for interaction have become ornamental. The teachers themselves did not place the teaching profession on the top of the ladder of various professions. It is this process that creates a sense of alienation among the rural teachers.

With regard to the problems of teachers such as appointment, promotion, transfers, retirement, housing, etc., the responses indicated the general dissatifaction with the present educational management. In respect of recruitment they preferred government management to Panchayti Raj control. In the case of transfers they felt that the norms have not been uniformly applied. In matter of promotion many of them felt that the gap is too wide and the basis of promotion not sound. They also complained about other facilities like proper housing in the villages. Thus, they were found frustrated with the overall management.

About the relevance of present education, they do not seem to have a clear-cut idea. However, livelihood, awareness and knowledge are stated to be the objectives of education. About the books, the teachers thought that they are not relevant to the future life of the children. In the place of the present education they pleaded for technical and vocational education. They were of the opinion that the existing education was not at all helpful and accessible to rural poor. They traced poverty and backwardness as root causes for non-availment of the existing educational facilities and large scale drop-outs. Absence of facilities and unattractive conditions in the school, according to the teachers, aggravated the problem further.

As the present practice does not include the teachers' participation in preparation of the text-books, they pleaded for greater involvement of the teachers in this process. The teachers also thought that the teaching methods and training of the teachers have been neither realistic nor academically sound. Regarding the role of the teachers' unions, they were largely dissatisfied. They expect the unions to play a larger role than what they have been doing at present. They suggested that unions can take upon the responsibility of ensuring better rapport between the teacher and the government on the one hand and the teacher and the community in general on the other. On the whole the teachers opined that the educational administration has been non-participative in nature and socially not relevant in character.

The silver lining in the whole analysis is the general value disposition of the teachers. The investigation revealed that they share broadly the democratic values and opined that education should be extended to all the sections and more so to the rural poor. They also felt that right type of education can play a crucial role in the development of the society. Except for this brighter side, in all respects their responses indicated the gloomy side of rural education.

Students constitute the heart of administration. An analysis of problems and perceptions of rural students presents a different dimension of educational administration. Among many problems that the rural students face more important one seems to be the problem of distance and transport. As the students come from different and far off villages, they have to commute from one kilometre to ten kilometres. They expressed several difficulties in walking the long distances. This obviously knocks away their leisure and they get so tired that they cannot concentrate on their studies, nor can participate in extra curricular activities like games, NCC and Scout. Contrary to the general belief that students do not earn while learning and lack dignity of labour, the study indicated that quite a number of students participate in agricultural operations and assist the parents in a number of activities. A few students from poorer families do take up even daily wage labour during the vacation.

With regard to the school timings, and the present scheme of vacation, a large number of them were in favour of the present arrangement. In respect of facilities while the students largely reported that they do have certain facilities in their school, they have complaints in matters of library, laboratory, toilet and drinking water. The responses indicate that most of these facilities do not exist. Even in respect of financial assistance, while the Scheduled Caste students and a few from the backward castes were getting the scholarships, a large majority of the students even from poorer sections were not covered by any of these schemes.

In respect of the teacher-student relations, while the teachers expressed dissatisfaction as pointed out earlier, the students were not negatively disposed towards the teachers. There has not been much of caning and punishment. It is interesting to note that the students were found interested in those subjects which are taught well. The teachers of those subjects were also warm and informal. The students appreciated the teachers using maps and illustrations while teaching. They also liked the teachers who use humour and occasionally crack jokes. With regard to their future plans, most of them proposed to study some technical short-term course, although about one fourth of them proposed to study professional courses like engineering and medicine. Most of them were conscious of their economic limitations and limited opportunities to pursue higher education.

The students pointed out poverty and economic backwardness as the principal causes for illiteracy in the villages. This is the reason, according to them, that accounts for a number of boys from their age group remaining outside the school or drop-out in the middle. A few responses indicated that the social practices like early marriages, pressure of work either in house or in the field also account for this phenomenon.

The socio-economic profile of students indicate that only 45 per cent of them come from the agricultural background. This includes 6 per cent of the children from the labour households. A majority of the students come either from artisan castes or modern type of professions. For 23 per cent of the children belong to the families dependent on traditional caste occupations, and another one-third come from the families largely belonging to the formal sector or those working in the modern professions. Although the agricultural labour constitute bulk of the populution, children from those families were negligible. It is this factor that explains the difficulties inherent in the universalisation of education in rural sector. And those rural boys who are in the school system feel handicapped and the opportunities for development of their skills and personality are limited.

The attitudes and perceptions of parents reveal that most of them were sending their children with a hope that they would get jobs in the organised sector. They were found favouring vocational education such as tailoring, motor mechanic, poultry, welding, etc., at school level itself. The parents were against their children doing manual labour even in the event of it fetching more income than mental labour. They felt that mental labour is more secure and comfortable. This type of value system is the counter-productive effect of education on rural work ethic.

An analysis of opinions of parents revealed that parents from smaller villages have difficulty in putting the children in the schools. The small villages are devoid of educational facilities. Most of the poor parents were not able to send the children to the school and have been facing economic difficulties. This is also true of certain lower middle class parents who were found dropping their children from studies because of economic difficulties and demands of agricultural and traditional caste occupations. Most of the illiterate children belong to poor families who cannot afford to send them to school. On the contrary, the children are pressed into work at a tender age to eke out their livelihood. The ill-health and lack of interest on the part of children accounts for a stagnation. Most of parents were neither satisfied with the way the schools have been functioning nor with the quality and quantum of assistance from the government. Intimate school-community relations were also absent. There was hardly any interaction between the teachers and the villagers. This indicates the weak community base for rural educational system.

The attitudes of village elite towards rural education are almost identical with that of the parents. They were also found dissatisfied with the existing facilities and the way the teachers have been working. The elite also maintained that school community interaction has been very poor. For the problems of inadequate coverage, drop-outs and stagnation, they traced the cause to poverty. The pattern of responses broadly indicates that elite do not evince much interest in matters of rural education, although they were favourably disposed towards universalisation of education.

The perception and attitudes of the parents and elite broadly indicate that the existing facilities were quite inadequate. The education is introducing a negative work ethic opposed to the dignity of labour. The poverty and backwardness are pointed out as the main constraints on the universalisation of education. The elite do not seem to be taking any interest for attainment of this goal. Given the present educational set-up and its linkages with the elite and their interaction, goals of universalisation of education appears to be a remote possibility.

The responses from the teachers, students, parents, and elite point out economic conditions of the rural poor as the main cause for children remaining out-side the school system. The mid-day meal scheme can be considered as one of the appropriate measures to overcome the problem. The scheme aims at universalisation of education and arresting the propensity for drop-outs. It is because of the importance of the scheme, it is analysed in the present investigation and the findings are presented.

An examination of the operation of the scheme in the three villages revealed that in the single teacher school, it is not only that the scheme had no positive impact but the teacher who used to spend some time in teaching became busy with the management of mid-day meal. The villagers complained of pilferages both by the cook and the teacher. The scheme did not take care of even the minimum requirements like water for drinking purposes, a protected shelter for eating the food, and a little care in creating the necessary hygiene both at the cooking and eating places. In the upper primary school, while the problems were identical, they had some different dimensions. The one problem they faced was the problem of untouchability. While Harijans insisted on being included in the whole-mid-day meal operations, the upper castes did not allow the children to take part in the meal. In the third village while they eliminated Harijans very intelligently, they faced a different type of crisis. Since the upper primary school has been part of secondary school, there were fourteen teachers. It is the 'politics' of the teachers that affected the scheme adversely. Thus, the experience in all the three villages sharply revealed the inadequacies in terms of manpower and infrastructure, stranglehold of traditional value set-up and the divisions and factions among the teachers and their manipulations.

Regarding the mid-day meal scheme a further investigation has been made into the attitudes and perceptions of the parents, elite and teachers to gain a deeper insight into the dynamics of such an important measure intended for universalisation of education. The responses of parents indicate that only about five per cent of the parents sent their children to the school because of the scheme. The attitudes towards mid-day meal programme were sharply divided. While the parents from lower middle and poorer classes were positive, the parents from upper middle and rich were negatively disposed towards the scheme. While parents from the poorer classes suggested improvement in the scheme, the parents from the upper castes and classes pleaded for winding up of the scheme and diversion of funds for building construction and further strengthening of the infrastructure.

An analysis of the elite responses also revealed similar trends that were seen in the case of parents. The elite agreed that the strength of students in the school increased, but they felt that the provisions given for meal were inadequate. They admitted that caste feelings were operating very actively. They highlighted a number of operational difficulties in the management of the scheme. In their overall response while a section of the elite pleaded for continuance and improvement in the scheme, another section advocated for the abandonment of the scheme. The sharp division in the opinions and attitudes are rooted in their socio-economic status in the rural society.

The teachers—another vital component of rural education-took a more bitter and negative attitudes towards the scheme. The teachers like the elite agreed that mid-day meal has a positive impact on the attendance and over-all improvement in the student strength of the school. However, they observed that the boys were found more interested in the scheme than in education. The teachers also thought that the infrastructure to manage the scheme was inadequate and the quantities supplied insufficient. They personally felt that the scheme adversely affected the teaching community and added a lot of physical burden to their work and a new tension in work place. A large number of teachers pleaded for abandonment of the scheme on the ground that it has not been well thought over and properly planned. The scheme, however, was abandoned by the government on the grounds of corruption and unsatisfactory implementation.

The analysis of a well intentioned public measures to universalise education, indicates how inadequate planning and hasty implementation can defeat the purpose for which it is initiated. The conception of the scheme was defective as it has not taken several factors into account, inspite of earlier experience with a similar scheme. The implementation floundered because of inadequate infrastructure and weak support from the upper strata. This is one example where one can notice the cob-webs of rural cultural set up, and their adverse impact on a policy.

The unhelpful environmental set-up, unsuitable administrative system, weak social base, inadequate infrastructure, unhappy teaching community, indifferent elite render rural education largely ineffective. Absence of proper planning, irrelevant curriculum, long distances, inhibit the fuller growth of the rural children. The ubiquitous poverty, pressure of agricultural or household work not only retain the students outside the system but give rise to the phenomenon of drop-outs. The existing educational strategy is too weak to cope with these complex problems. Consequently the gap between promise and performance is bound to be wide as far as universalisation of education is concerned.

Bibliography

Reports and Acts

Government of Andhra Pradesh: *Working Paper on Panchayati Raj Institutions*, State Committee on Panchayati Raj Institutions, Hyderabad, 1980.

Government of Andhra Pradesh: *Andhra Pradesh District Gazetteers*, Warangal, Hyderabad, 1976.

Government of Andhra Pradesh: *The Andhra Pradesh Panchayat Samithis and Zilla Parishads Act*, Hyderabad, 1978.

Government of Andhra Pradesh : *Andhra Pradesh Gram Panchayat Act, 1964*, Hyderabad, 1978.

Government of India: *India A Reference Annual 1974*, Research and Reference Division, Ministry of Information and Broadcasting, Delhi, 1974.

Government of India : *Problem of Extension of Primary Education in Rural Areas*, Programme Evaluation Organisation, Planning Commission, New Delhi, 1965.

Government of India: Report of the Education Commission 1964-1966, *Education and National Development*, Ministry of Education, New Delhi, 1966.

Government of India : *Report of the Secondary Education Commission (1952-53)*, Ministry of Education and Social Welfare, Government of India, New Delhi, 1972.

Government of India : *Challenge of Education—A Policy Perspective*, Ministry of Education, New Delhi, August, 1985.

Government of India : *National Policy on Education 1986* : Ministry of Human Resource Development (Dept. of Education), New Delhi, May, 1986.

Government of India : *The Gazetteer of India, Vol. IV, Administration and Public Welfare*, Ministry of Education and Social Welfare, Government of India, New Delhi, 1978.

Ramachandran, G. : *Report of Basic Education Evaluation Committee*, Ministry of Education and Scientific Research, Government of India, 1957.

Report of the Committee on the Establishment of an Open University : *Towards an Open Learning System*, Hyderabad, 1982.

Books

Abu Bekar, M. : *The Union and the States in Education : A Study in Educational Finance and Planning*, Shabd Sanchar, New Delhi, 1976.

Andrew W. Halping (Ed.) : *Administrative Theory in Education*, The MacMillan Company, New York, 1967.

Aparna Basu : *The Growth of Education and Political Development in India 1898-1920*, Oxford University Press, Delhi, 1970.

Abba Sayalu, Y.B.: *Scheduled Caste Elite : A Study of Scheduled Caste Elite in Andhra Pradesh*, Booklinks Corporation, Hyderabed, 1978.

Addaval, S.B. (Ed) : *The Third India Year Book of* Education : *Educational Research*, NCERT, New Delhi, 1968.

Anderson, C.A. and M.J. Bowman : *Education and Economic Development*, Frank Cass, London, 1971.

Alva Myrdal : "The Power of Education", in Emmet John Hughs (ed.,) *Education in World Perspective*, Lancer Books, New York, 1965.

Aggarwal, J.C. : *National Policy on Education*, Arya Book Depot, New Delhi, 1979.

Aggarwal, J.C. : *Development and Planning of Modern Education with Special Reference to India*, Vikas Publishing House, New Delhi, 1982.

Balaramulu, Ch.: *Organisation and Working of a Small Farmers Development Agency—Case Study* (Ph. D Thesis), Dept. of Public Administration, Kakatiya University, Warangal. 1980.

Biswas, Dutt Sunnittee and R.P. Singhal: *The New Educational Pattern in India*, Vikas Publishing House, Delhi, 1976.

Bhatnagar and Gunam Saran, *Education and Social Change : A Study in Some Rural Communities in Punjab*, The Minarva Associates, Calcutta, 1972.

Bhatia, S.C. : *Education and Socio-Cultural Disadvantage*, Xerxes Publications, Delhi, 1982.

Bose, P.K. and others: "Educational Facilities Available in Higher Secondary Schools of West Bengal (1963-64)", Calcutta University, 1965. in M.B. Buch (Ed.) *Second Survey of Research in Education*, Society for Educational Research and Development, Baroda, 1970.

Brij Raj Chauhan, G. Narayan and T.R. Singh : *Scheduled Castes and Education*, Anu Publications, Meerat, 1975.

Buch, M.B., (Ed.,) : *A Survey of Research in Education*, Centre of Advanced Study in Education, M.S. University of Baroda, Baroda, 1974.

Buch, M.B. (Ed.) : *Second Survey of Research in Education 1972-1978*, Society for Educational Research and Development, Baroda, 1979.

Chourasia, G. : *Challenges and Innovations in Education*, Sterling Publishers, New Delhi, 1977.

Charles Jeffries : *Illiteracy : A World Problem*, Pall Mall Press London, 1967.

Citizens for Democracy : *Education for Our People : A Policy Frame. for the Development of Education (1978-87)*, Allied Publishers, Bombay, 1978.

Dharni, P. Sinha: *Descriptive-cum-Critical Study of Education System in Andhra Pradesh*, Administrative Staff College of India, Hyderabad, 1976, (cyclo).

Dharni, P. Singh : *Descriptive-cum-Analytical Study of Nagaland Education System*, Administrative Staff College of India, Hyderabad, 1976. (cyclo).

Denis, Lawton : *Education and Social Justice*, Sage Publications, London, 1977.

Desai, A.R. : *Rural Sociology in India*, Popular Prakashan, Bombay, 1978.

Desai, A.R. : "Social Change and Educational Policy", in M.S. Gore and Others (ed.,), *Papers in the Sociology of Education in India*, NCERT, New Delhi, 1975.

Don Adams : *Education and Modernisation in Asia*, Addison Wesley Publishing Company, London, 1970.

Eshnul Haq : *Education and Political Culture in India*, Sterling Publishers, New Delhi, 1981.

Ghosh, S.C. (Ed.) : *Educatianal Strategies in Developing Countries*, Sterling Publishers, New Delhi, 1976.

Gunnar, Myrdal : *Asian Drama – An Inquiry into the Poverty of Nations*, Abridged by Seth S. King, Allen Lane, London, 1972.

Gunnar Myrdal: "Educational Reform in Under Developed Countries," A.B. Shah (Ed.) *The Social Context of Education : Essays in Honour of J.P. Naik*, Allied Publishers, New Delhi, 1978.

Gore, M.S., and others (Ed.) : *Papers in the Sociology of Education in India*, NCERT, New Delhi, 1967.

Goel, S.C., *Education and Economic Growth in India*, The MacMillan Company of India Ltd., Delhi, 1975.

Ganguly, S.N.: *Tradition, Modernity and Development: A Study in Contemporary Indian Society*, MacMillan Company of India, Delhi, 1977.

Gopinathan Nair, P.R.: *Primary Education, Population Growth and Socio-Economic Change*, Allied Publishers, New Delhi, 1981.

Gandhi, M.K. : *My views on Education*, Bharatiya Vidya Bhavan, Bombay, 1970.

Haragopal, G. : *Administrative Leadership and Rural Development in India*, Light & Life Publishers, New Delhi, 1980.

Iqbal Narain: "Rural Local Politics and Primary School Management" in Rudolph & Rudolph (Ed.) *Education and Politics in India: Studies in Organisation, Society and Policy*: Harvard University Press, Cambridge, 1972.

Iqbal Narain, K.C. Pande and Mohan Lal Sarma: *Panchayati Raj and Educational Administration*, Aalakli Publishers, Jaipur, 1976.

International Commission on the Development of Education: *Learning to be*, UNESCO, Sterling Publishers, New Delhi, 1973.

Inamdar, N.R.: *Educational Administration in the Zilla Parishads in Maharashtra*, Popular Prakashan, Bombay, 1974,

International Encyclopaedia of Social Sciencess: The Mac Millan Company and the Free Press, Vol. 4, 1968.

Julian, E.. Butter Worth and Howard A. Dawson: *The Modern Rural School*, McGraw Hill, New York, 1952.

John W., Hanson and Cole S. Brem Beck: *Education and the Development of Nations*, Holt, Rinehart and Winston, New York, 1966.

John Vaizey: *Education for Tomorrow*, Penguin, London, 1966.

Joshi, R.N.: *Education—Elsewhere and Here*, Bharatiya Vidya Bhavan, Bombay, 1979.

Kishore Gandhi: *Issues and Choices in Higher Education: A Sociological Analysis*, B.R. Publishing Corporation, Delhi, 1977.

Kidd, J.R.: *Education for Perspective*, Indian Education Association, New Delhi, 1969.

Kochhar, S.K.: *Pivotal Issues in Indian Education*, Sterling, New Delhi, 1981.

Kamat, A.R.: *The Educational Situation and other Essays on Education*, People's Publishing House, New Delhi, 1973.

Lamshmana Swamy Mudaliar, A.: *Education in India*, Asia Publishing House, Bombay, 1960.

Louis Malassis: *The Rural World: Education and Development*, Croom Helm, London, 1976.

Mukherji, S.N. (Ed.,): *Administration of Education in India.* Acharya Book Depot, Baroda, 1962.

Mukherjee, R.K. : *The Social Structure of Values*, S. Chand & Company, New Delhi, 1964.

Majid Rahnema, "Iran," in Suresh Gosh (Ed) : *Educational Strategies in Developing Countries*, Sterling Publishers, New Delhi, 1976.

Naik, J.P. : "Education", in Dubc S.C. (Ed.), *India Since Independencc*, Vikas Publishing House, New Delhi, 1977.

Naik, J.P.: *Policy and Performance in Indian Education 1947-74*, Dr. K.G. Saiyidain Memorial Lectures, Dr. K.G. Saiyidain Memorial Trust, New Delhi, 1975.

Naik, J.P. : *The Single Teacher School* : *Studies in Education and Psychology*, Ministry of Education, Government of India, 1953.

Naik, J.P. *Educational Planning in India*, Allied Publishers, Bombay, 1965.

Naik, J.P. :*Education of the Scheduled Castes 1965-66*, Occasional Monograph, ICSSR, No. 6, New Delhi.

Naik, J.P. : *Elementary Education in India* : *A Promise to Keep*. Allied Publishers, Bombay, 1975.

Naik, J.P. : *Equality, Quality and Quaniity* : *The Elusive Triangle in Indian Education*, Allied Publishers, New Delhi, 1975.

Naik, J.P. : *Education in the Fourth Plan* : *Review and Perspective*, Nachiketa Publications, Bombay, 1968.

Naik, J.P. : *The National Education Policy 1947-1978*, Ministry of Education and Social Welfare, Government of India. New Delhi, 1979.

Naik, J.P. : *Some Perspectives on Non-Formal Education*, Allied Publishers, New Delhi, 1977.

Nural Hasan, S. : *Challenges in Education, Culture and Social Welfare*, Allied Publishers, Bombay, 1977.

Nirmalya Bagchi : *Cheep Poison*, Chalti Duniya, Calcutta, 1974.

Niblett, W.R. : *Essential Education*, University of London, London, 1955.

NCERT : *The Indian Year Book of Education 1964, Second Year Book-Elementary Education*, New Delhi, 1964.

Oldhan. J.N. : *Village Education in India : The Report of Commission of Enquiry*, Oxford University Press, London, 1922.

Paulo Freire : *Pedagogy of the Oppressed*, Penguin Books, New York, 1977.

Paulo Freire : *Cultural Action for Freedom*, Penguin Books, New York, 1977.

Paulo Freire : *Education : The Practice of Freedom*, Writers and Readers Publishing Co-operative, London, 1976.

Premi, M.K. : *Educational Planning in India : Implications of Population Trends*, Sterling Publishers, New Delhi, 1972.

Prem Kripal : *A Decade of Education in India*, Indian Book Company, Delhi, 1968.

Panchamukhi, P.R.: Financing of Primary Education in India". in *Primary and Work-Oriented Education*, NCERT, 1970.

Pandey, S.N. : *Education and Social Changes in Bihar (1900-1921) : A Survey of Social History of Bihar from Curzon to Non-Cooperation Movement*, Motilal Benarasidas, Delhi, 1976.

Rudolph & Rudolph (Ed.) : *Education and Politics in India : Studies in Organisation, Society and Policy*, Harvard University Press, Cambridge, 1972.

Rajagopal, M.V. : *Kothari Commission on School Education : A Recapitulation and Review*, Telugu Vidyardhi Prachuranalu, Machilipatnam, 1967.

Ratna, G. Revankar : *The Indian Constitution : A Case Study of Backward Classes*, Associate University Press, Canbury, New Jersey, 1941.

Ram Reddy, G. (Ed.,) : *Patterns of Panehayati Raj in India*, MacMillan Company of India, Madras, 1977.

Raju, V.B. : *Commentaries on the Constitution of India*, Eastern Book Company, Lucknow, 1973.

Rao, V.K.R.V. : *Education and Human Resource Development*, Allied Publishers, Bombay, 1966.

Rao, M.S. : "Education Social Stratification and Mobility," in M.S. Gore and others (ed.), *Papers in the Sociology of*

Education in India, NCERT, New Delhi, 1975.

Russell, Bertrand : *Education and the Social Order*, Unwin, London, 1977.

Russel, Bertrand : *On Education*, Unwin Books, London, 1971.

Raghunath Safaya : *Innovations and Latest Trends in Education*, The Associated Publishers, Ambala Contt., 1976.

Rajagopal, S. · "A Critical Study of English Curriculum at the Primary and Secondary Stages of Education in the Madras State (Tamil Nadu)" Ph. D., thesis, Annamalai University 1972, in M.B. Buch (Ed.), *A Survey of Research in Education, Centre for Advanced Study* in Education, M.S. University, Baroda, 1974.

Shri Prakash : *Educational System of India : An Econometric Study*, Concept Publishing Company, Delhi, 1977.

Satya, R.N. : *Innovations and Latest Trends in Education*, The Associated Publishers, Ambala Contt., 1976.

Sharma, G.S. : *Educational and Cultural Development of the Minorities—A Study in Social Effects of the Judicial Trends in India*, ICSSR, New Delhi, 1973.

Sachidananda : *The Harijan Elite*, Thomson Press, New Delhi, 1977.

Singh, M.M. : *The Constitution of India—Studies in Perspective* The World Press, Calcutta, 1975,

Siqueira, T.N. : *The Education of India-History and Problems*, Oxford University Press, London, 1952.

Sundaram, P.S. and A.B. Shah : *Education or Catastrophe* ? Vikas Publishing House, New Delhi, 1976.

Sateswari Saxena : *Education Planning in India : A Study in Approach and Methodology*, Sterling Publishers, New Delhi, 1974

Saini, S.K.: *Development of Education in India : Socio-Economic and Political Perspective*, Cosmo Publications, New Delhi, 1980

Stephen J. Knezevich : *Administration of Public Education* : Harper and Brothers, New York, 1962.

Shukla, P.D. : *Towards the New Pattern of Education in India*, Sterling Publishers, New Delhi, 1976.

Shipman, M.D. : *Education and Modernisation* : Faber and Faber London, 1971.

Shrimali, K.L. ; *A Search for Values in Indian Education*: Vikas Publishers, Delhi, 1974

Sreenivas Reddy G. : *Administration of Harijan Welfare Programmes : Case Study of a District in A. P.*, Dept. of Public Administration, Kakatiya University, 1981, (Ph.D., thesis).

Tiwari, D.D.: *Education at the Cross Roads*, Chugh Publications, Allahabad, 1975.

Tiwari, D.D. : *Thoughts on Education*, Chugh Publications, 1972.

The New Encyclopaedia of Britanica, Helen Hemingway Benton Chicago, Vol. 6, 1977.

UNESCO : *Progress of Literacy in Various Countries*, Paris, 1954.

Venkatasubramanian, K. : *Education and Learning in Andhra Uuder the East India Company*, N. Vidyaranya Swamy, Secunderabad, 1979.

Articles

Amiya Rao : "Primary Education—Problems and Purpose," *Economic and Political Weekly*, Vol. 15, No. 10 March, 1980, pp. 603-506.

Aikaa, Jacob : "Education and Politics in India", *Indian Journal of Adult Education*. Vol. 37, No. 1, 1976.

Arun Sinha : "Bihar Primary Education Made Attractive", *Economic and Political Weekly*, Vol. 12, Nos. 1 & 2, January 8, 1977.

Amba Roa, U.: "Higher Education and Occupational Mobility among the Scheduled Caste Youth", *Journal of Higher Education*, Vol. 1, Vol No. 3, Spring, 1973.

Asit Ray: " Education for the Elite", *Social Scientist*, Vol. 1, No. 9, April, 1973.

Aleyamma George: "Literacy : Doorway of Literacy", *Social Scientist*, Vol. 4/5, Nov/Dec., 1975.

Ashoka Thaper: "Education", *Seminar*, No. 108, August, 1968.

Bhatawdekar: " Economic Growth and Education in Japan", *Economic and Political Weekly*, Vol. 7, No. 35, August, 26, 1972.

Bhatawdaker: "Integration of Education and Economic Plan" *Economic and Political Weekly*, Vol. 6, No. 30-32, July, 1971.

Bhandari, R.K.: "Educational Development in the Seventh Five Year Plan, *New Frontiers in Education*, Vol. XIII, No. 4, October-December, 1983.

Baldev Singh : " Impact of Education on Farm Production", *Economic and Political Weekly*, Vol. 9, No. 39, September, 1974.

Bora, P.M.: "Teacher and the Local Boss", *Social Scientist*, Vol. 5, No. 3. October, 1976.

Brahm, P. Gupta: "Developing the Human Capital", *Seminar*, No. 71, July, 1965.

Chaudhuri, S.K.: "Educational Process in Rural Bengal—A Study of Four Villages", *Economic and Political Weekly*, Vol. 5, No. 6, February 7, 1970

Chander, P.C.: "Education for the Changing India", *Yojana*, Vol. 22 No. 12, July 1, 1978.

Charles, K.J. : "Education and Poverty in South Asia", *Khadigramodyog*, Vol. 22, No. 2, November, 1975.

Deshpande, J.V.: "Education : Pacifier-for Some", *Economic and Political Weekly* : Vol. 9, No. 16, April 20, 1974.

Datar, B.N.: "Literate Labour", *Seminar*, No. 18, February, 1961.

Gopinatham Nair: "Education and Socio-Economic Change in Kerala 1893-1947", *Social Scientist* : Vol. 4, No. 8, March 1976, pp. 28-43.

Gopinatham Nair, P.R.: "Effective Cost of Primary Education in India", *Economic and Political Weekly*, Vol. 11. No. 38, September 18, 1976.

Gail Omvedt: "Whither Scheduled Castes", *The Illustrated Weekly of India* , Vol. C 33, November, 18-24, 1979.

Gopalan : "Educational Institutions and Rural Development", *Kurukshetra*, Vol. 25, No. 12, March 16, 1977.

Harichandran, C. : "Elementary Education Through Panchayati Raj in Tamil Nadu", *Kurukshetra*, Vol. 23, No. 18, June 16, 1975.

Haragopal, G. and G. Sudarshan : "Rural Adult Literacy : An Enquiry into the Attitudes", *Indian Journal of Adult Education*, Vol. 47, October, 1978.

Haragopal, G. : "Literacy and Education" *Seminar*, No. 235, March, 1979.

Iravati Karve "Education and Social Change", *Economic and Political Weekly*, Vol. 3, Nos. 1 and 2, January, 1980.

Jetley, S. : "Education and Occupational Mobility : A U.P. Village, *Economic and Political Weekly*, Vol. 4, No. 17, April 26, 1969.

Jog Paul and Goyatri Moorthy : "Humanising Education", *Yojana*, Vol. 20, No. 23, January, 1977.

Joosten, A.M. : "Pre-primary Education in Developing Democracies", *Yojana*, Vol. 15 No. 17, September 6, 1970.

Karuna Ahmad: "Towards a Study of Education and Social Change", *Economic and Political Weekly*, Vol. 14, No. 4, January 27, 1979, pp. 157-164.

Kamat, A.R.: "Primary Education : Participation and Wastage", *Economic and Political Weekly*, Vol. 7, No. 18, April 29, 1972.

Kamat, A.R.: "The Educational Situation", *Economic and Political Weekly*, Vol. 7, No. 26, January 24, 1972.

Kamat, A.R.: "Educational Progress in Rural Maharashtra", *Economic and Political Weekly*, Vol. 3, No. 40, October 5, 1968.

Kamat, A.R. : "Woman's Education and Social Change in India", *Social Scientist*, Vol. 5, No. 1 August, 1976.

Kusum, K. Premi : "Educational Opportunities for the Scheduled Caste", *Economic and Political Weekly*, Vol. 9, No. 45 & 46, November 9, 1974.

Kalyan Choudari : "Education : Calcutta's Primary School", *Economic and Political Weekly*, Vol. 12, No. 3, January, 15, 1977.

Karve, D.D.: "Unfashionable Views on Education", *Economic and Political Weekly*, Vol. 12, No, 10, March 5, 1977.

Krishna Kumar: "Primary Education : Problem and Purpose—A Comment", *Economic and Political Weekly*, Vol. 15 No. 17, April 26, 1980.

Kumaresh Chakravarthy: "Education in the Fifth Plan", *Social Scientist*, Vol. 1, No. 3, October, 1972.

Kartar Singh Sangwan: "Some Reflections on Higher Education", *Social Scientist*, Vol. 1, No. 7, February, 1973.

Kistaiah, M. K.: Seeta Rama Rao and G. Sudarshanam, "Interim Report of the Study Team on Drop-outs at Primary School Level," Department of Public Administration, Kakatiya University, Warangal, 1980 (Mimeographed).

Leon, E Clark: "A Change in Approach", *Seminar*, No. 71, July, 1965.

Malcolm S., Adiseshaiah: "Education : Futility of Aggregative Approach", *Economic and Political Weekly*, Vol. 7, No. 42, October, 14 1972.

Malcolm S. Adiseshaiah: "New Education Pattern : Opportunity to face Basic Issues", *Economic and Political Weekly*, No. 49, Vol. 12 December 3, 1977.

Maria Mies: "Paulo Freire's Method of Education, Conscientisation in Latin America", *Economic and Political Weekly*, Vol. 8, No. 39, September 29, 1973.

Menon, P.S.K.: "Post Matric Scholarships for Scheduled Castes and Scheduled Tribes Students", *Journal of Higher Education*, Vol. 1, No. 2, Autumn 1975.

Mehta, S.R.: "Role of School Teacher in Village Leadership", *Kurukshetra*, Vol. 21, No. 5, December 1, 1872.

Mohan Thamp: "The Educational Thought of Paulo Freire", *Social Scientist*, Vol. 2, No. 1, August 1973.

Moinuddin Herris: "The Problem", *Seminar*, No. 71, July 1965.

Mittal, O.P.: "Problem of the Young—need for an Appropriate Policy", *Yojana*, Vol. 15, No. 17, September, 6, 1970.

Methur, V.S.: "Adult Education in India, *Yojana*, Vol. 15, Nos 1, 2 & 3, February 21, 1971.

Malavika Karkar: "Higher Education and the Scheduled

Castes", *Journal of Higher Education*, Vol. 1, No. 2, Autumn, 1975.

Nain Chandra Joshi: "The Education that Failed", *Yojana* Vol. 22, No. 12, July, 1978.

Nayar, D.P.: "Social Justice and Education", *Yojana*, Vol. 19, No. 3, March 1, 1975.

Nayar, D. P.: "India Launches International Education Year", *Yojana*, Vol. 15, No. 17, September 6, 1970.

Narayana, G.: "Rule-Making for Scheduled Castes", *Economic and Political Weekly*, Vol. 15, No. 8, February 23, 1980.

Naik, J. P.: "Educational Administration in Urban Areas", *Indian Journal of Public Administration*, Vol. 14, No. 3, July-September, 1968.

Pandit, H. N.: "Financing of School Education", *Economic and Political Weekly*, Vol. 7, Nos. 31, 32 & 33, August 1972.

Premi, M. K.: "Planning Educational Programmes", *Economic and Political Weekly*, Vol. 3, No. 8, February 24, 1968.

Parichaya: "Educational Research and Training", *Economic and Political Weekly*, Vol. 3, No. 32, August 10, 1968.

Panchamukhi, P.R.: "Decision-Making in Education", *Economic and Political Weekly*, Vol. 5, Nos. 4 & 5, January, 1970.

"Primary Education in India, Documents", *New Frontiers in Education*, Vol. X, No. 1, January-March, 1980.

Pranab Mukherjee: "Eradicating Illiteracy", *Kurukshetra*, Vol. 21, No. 19, July, 1, 1973.

Pradeep Kumar Mehta: "Education in Rural India", *Kurukshetra*, Vol. 26, No. 1, October 2, 1977.

Prasad, R.C.: "Educational Development", *Seminar*, No. 167, July, 1968.

Padmanabhan: "Cost Analysis in Educational Administration" *Yojana*, Vol. 15, No. 17, September 6, 1970.

Paul, Guerileire: "Area of Departure", *Seminar*, No. 158, October, 1972.

Pandit, Nalini : "Literacy Among Scheduled Castes of Maharashtra", *Economic and Political Weekly*, May 25, 1974.

Rudolph and Rudolph: "Regional Patterns of Education",

Economic and Political Weekly, Vol. 4, No. 26, June 28, 1969.

Rudolph and Rudolph: "Standards in Democratic Higher Education", *Economic and Political Weekly*, Vol. 5, Nos. 4 & 5, January, 1970.

Romesh Diwan: "Development, Education and the Poor: Context of South Asia", *Economic and Political Weekly*, Vol. 12, No. 9 February 3, 1977.

Rais Ahmad: "New Education Pattern : Hair Splitting by Privileged", *Economic and Political Weekly*, Vol. 12, No. 49 December 3, 1977.

Rajagopal, M.V.: "Planning for the Eighties", *Indian Education* Vol. X, Nos. 1 & 2, April-May, 1980.

Rudolfo, Baron Castro: "Illiteracy ! World Problem", *Kurukshetra*, Vol. 21, No. 10, February 16, 1973,

Rakesh Hooja: "Rural Education in Ajmer District", *Kurukshetra*, Vol. 25, No. 19, July, 1977.

Rakesh Hooja "Rural Education and Development", *Kuru-Kshetra*, Vol. 15, No. 10, February 16, 1977.

Rudra, K.K. and Rastogi, S.P.: "Education and Employment", *Yojana*, Vol. 21, No. 8, May 15, 1977.

Ruddar Datt: "Education under the Sixth Plan", *Yojana*, Vol. 22, No. 12, July 1, 1978.

Ramaswamy, A.S.: "Education for High Produetivity", *Kurukshetra*, Vol. 20, No. 2, October 16, 1971.

"Rural Education and Training in Tanzania", *Kurukshetra*, Vol. 19 No. 19, July 1, 1971.

Ramachadra Raj, G.: "Indian Public Schools", (Book Review) *Social Scientist*, Vol. 3, No. 6/7, January/February, 1975.

Rasid Azar: "Education Perspective," *Seminar*, No. 88, December 1976.

Rao, B.R.K.: "Education and Welfare", *Khadigramodyog*, Vol. 20, No. 8, May 1974.

Rabinson, Joan: "Education", *Social Scientist*, Vol. 5, Nos. 10/11, May-June, 1977.

Satish Saberwal: "Education and Inequality", *Economic and Political Weekly*, Vol. 7, Nos. 5, 6 & 7, February 22, 1972.

Satish Saberwal: "Education, Inequality Industrialisation," *Journal of Higher Education*, Vol. 1, No.2, Autumn, 1975.

Suma Chitnis: "Education for Equality, Case of Scheduled Castes, *Economic and Political Weekly*, Vol. 7, Nos. 31, 32 & 33, August, 1972.

Suma Chitnis: "Education of the Scheduled Castes," *Journal of Higher Education*, Vol. 1, No. 2, Autmn, 1975.

Shali, K.R., "Expenditure on Elementary Education : 1950-51 to 1960-61", *Economic and Political Weekly*, Vol. 4, No. 47 November 22, 1969.

Shukla, S.: "Priorities in Educational Policy", *Economic and Political Weekly*, Vol. 6, Nos. 30 & 32, July 1971.

Surinder Suri: "New Perspective", *Seminar*, No. 177, May 1974

Singh, Raja Roy: "Educational Administration in India", *Indian Journal of Public Administration*, Vol. 9, No. 3, (Supplement)

Srivastava, R.K. : "Administrative Problems in Educational Planning", *Indian Journal of Public Administration*, Vol. 10, No. 4, October-December 1964.

"School Education in India—Outlook", *The Hindu*, July 26, 1978.

Susila Bai: "Lower Primary School Drop-outs", *Deccan Chronicle*, June 10, 1979.

Staley, Eugene: "Towards a More Work-oriented Schooling", *Economic and Political Weekly* Special Number August 1972.

Tomcha Singh: "Education", *Kurukshetra*, Vol. 25, No. 20, July 16, 1977.

Tara Ali Baigh: "The Child in Rural India", *Kurukshetra*, Vol. 22, No. 4, Nov. 16, 1973.

Tiwari, R.S. : "Adult Education Programme—Some Apprehensions", *Indian Journal of Adult Education*, October, 1978.

"The Child in India : A Statistical Abstract", *Yojana*, Vol. 20 November 1-14, 1976.

"The Purpose of Education—One Teacher's Point of View", *D. K. News Letter*, Vol. 4, No. 20, December 20, 1978.

Uma Rama Swamy: "Scheduled Castes in Andhra : Some Aspects of Social Change", *Economic and Political Weekly*, Vol. 9, No. 21, July 20, 1974.

Vasantha, Surya: "Breathing Life into Primary Education", *Economic and Political Weekly*, Vol. 12, No. 18, April 30, 1977.

Venkataramaiah, P. and G. S. Rajguru: "Impact of Schooling on Scientific Farming", *Kurukshetra,* Vol. 23, No. 18, June 16, 1975.

Vimal Chandra: "Constitutional Safeguards', *Seminar,* (Symposium on School), No. 71, July 1965.

Vashi, D.G.: "Educational Planning in India", *Yojana,* Vol. 18 No. 6, April 15, 1974,

"Welfare Measures for the Backward", *Yojana,* Vol. 20, No. 23 January, 1977.

"Welfare of Weaker Sections in Andhra Pradesh", *Kurukshetra,* Vol. 25, No. 2, October 16, 1976.

Index